Teacher's Book

CAE
Practice Tests 2
TEACHER'S BOOK

Louise Hashemi

CAMBRIDGE
UNIVERSITY PRESS

Published by the Press Syndicate of the University of Cambridge
The Pitt Building, Trumpington Street, Cambridge CB2 1RP
40 West 20th Street, New York, NY 10011-4211, USA
10 Stamford Road, Oakleigh, Victoria 3166, Australia

© Cambridge University Press 1994

First published 1994

Printed in Great Britain at the University Press, Cambridge

ISBN 0 521 44888 3 Teacher's Book
ISBN 0 521 44886 7 Student's Book
ISBN 0 521 44889 1 Cassettes

Copyright
The law allows a reader to make a single copy of part of a book for purposes of private study. It does not allow the copying of entire books or the making of multiple copies of extracts. Written permission for any such copying must always be obtained from the publisher in advance.

GO

Contents

Introduction 1

Question aims and formats 3

Marking and grading 8
Assessment and marking of Paper 2 Writing 9
Assessment and marking of Paper 5 Speaking 19

Preparing students for CAE 22

Practice Test 1
Paper 1   Reading   26
Paper 2   Writing   26
Paper 3   English in Use   26
Paper 4   Listening   27
Paper 5   Speaking   32

Practice Test 2
Paper 1   Reading   35
Paper 2   Writing   35
Paper 3   English in Use   35
Paper 4   Listening   36
Paper 5   Speaking   42

Practice Test 3
Paper 1   Reading   45
Paper 2   Writing   45
Paper 3   English in Use   46
Paper 4   Listening   47
Paper 5   Speaking   53

Practice Test 4
Paper 1   Reading   56
Paper 2   Writing   56
Paper 3   English in Use   56
Paper 4   Listening   57
Paper 5   Speaking   63

Acknowledgements

The assessment criteria on pp. 18 and 21 and the sample answer sheets in the Student's Book are reproduced by kind permission of the University of Cambridge Local Examinations Syndicate.

Introduction

What is the CAE?

The Certificate in Advanced English (CAE) is an examination in general English introduced by the University of Cambridge Local Examinations Syndicate (UCLES) in 1991. It is one of a range of examinations from elementary level (the Preliminary English Test) through intermediate level (the First Certificate in English) to proficiency standard (the Certificate of Proficiency in English). It is intended to offer students a high-level qualification in the language, which for many will be a significant final achievement, or to prepare them for the more academically demanding CPE. This set of four complete practice tests is aimed to give students help in developing the skills needed to attempt CAE.

Level

The level of English reflected in these practice tests, as in the examination, assumes that the student will have achieved a similar standard to a C grade in the Cambridge First Certificate before beginning to prepare for CAE. The content of the test materials is chosen to encourage the students to practise the skills which they will need in their jobs and careers, so the practice tests lay stress on real world tasks wherever this is appropriate. For those students who want to continue their study of the language and take the CPE, the tests offer a level of lexis and structure which will help develop the linguistic skills needed for this higher level examination.

As in the actual examination, the language level of the instructions, the texts and the individual questions of these practice tests fall within a range from that of First Certificate to a level about two-thirds of the way towards the CPE.

Authentic texts

Most of the texts used in the examination come from authentic sources and the practice tests reflect both this and the resulting increase in language level of the stimulus material. However, care has been taken not to test lexis or structure which falls outside the level unless there are enough clues in the texts to help the students. The amount of material used in this way is similar to that in the actual examination. The texts have been chosen from a wide range of authentic non-fiction sources such as magazines, newspapers and periodicals, information leaflets, guide books and brochures, in order to encourage teachers and students to become accustomed to using 'real' English sources in the classroom. We hope that the materials are interesting and stimulating for teacher and student alike.

Introduction

The structure of CAE

The examination is divided into five paper components, each of which carries 20 per cent of the total marks. The papers are as follows:

Paper 1	Reading	1 hour 15 minutes
Paper 2	Writing	2 hours
Paper 3	English in Use	1 hour 30 minutes
Paper 4	Listening	45 minutes (approx.)
Paper 5	Speaking	15 minutes (approx.)

Question aims and formats

Paper 1 Reading

The Reading paper consists of four authentic texts drawn from a range of British and international publications. Most of the texts are laid out in their original form and are, as far as possible, unedited. Some texts have been shortened in order to adhere to the word limit imposed by the specification (3,000 words for Paper 1). Texts are sometimes made up from a series of shorter pieces. Fifteen minutes reading time is given in which students can familiarise themselves with the questions and texts before they start trying to answer.

There is a wide variety of text types, such as material from leaflets, newspapers and magazines. Visuals may be used and abbreviations or note form may occasionally be included when appropriate.

Teachers may feel that 3,000 words is a heavy reading load for students in an examination but the intention is to encourage students to develop different reading skills appropriate to the text and task. In particular, students should practise the skills of skimming and scanning texts for overall impression or specific information. These are real-world skills which the examination and these practice texts hope to develop.

More traditional reading skills (also exemplified in the CPE), such as interpreting the text for inference, attitude and style or deducing meaning from context are also a significant aim of the Reading paper.

The questions are various types of multiple choice, cloze (the 'gapped' text) or matching. There are about 40 questions in each test. The raw total is weighted so that it contributes 20 per cent to the total examination mark.

Sometimes the questions are printed before the text in order to show the students that they will need to scan the text for specific information. In this sort of task the student should expect to find that the questions do not necessarily follow the order of the text.

In other parts of the Reading paper the questions follow the text in the normal way and usually the questions follow the order of the text. Those questions which attempt to discover if the student understands the gist or overall impression of a text tend to come towards the end of a series of questions. In some cases more than one set of questions accompanies a text. It is part of the rationale for the CAE that question type, text layout and ordering of questions should reflect the natural aspects of reading competence.

Because this paper is marked by computer, the students are asked to record their answers in the form of letters of the alphabet on the optically marked sheet (OMR). This requires the student to pencil in a lozenge on a single sheet of A4 OMR, as in the reading component of FCE and CPE. It is important that the students use soft pencil as the OMR reader is not sensitive to pen or biro. If

Question aims and formats

a mistake is made, the student should carefully erase the mark with a rubber. Tipp-Ex should not be used.

As the students have only 75 minutes to complete the paper, it is probably not a good idea for them to transfer their answers to the OMR sheet at the end of the test. When using these practice tests, students may want to record their answers in the book or on a separate sheet of paper. Sample OMR sheets for Paper 1 are provided at the back of the Student's Book.

It is strongly recommended that students have plenty of practice with the OMR sheets so that they are not troubled by the mechanics of transferring their answers during the actual examination.

Paper 2   Writing

The Writing paper is divided into two sections carrying equal marks. In both Section A and Section B students are asked to do tasks based on materials drawn from a variety of sources including articles, notes and messages, letters, reports, reviews and instructions. Besides testing linguistic accuracy at an advanced level, the Writing paper aims to assess the student's ability to write in a register and style appropriate to the task and to present the work effectively. In each case the task is contextualised and the purpose and intended recipient of the piece of writing is given in order to encourage a well-focused response in a controlled context. It is essential for the student to comprehend fully the nature and detail of the task before attempting to tackle it. Students will lose marks if their answers do not fit the parameters laid down by the task. (See also p. 18 Writing – Assessment Criteria).

In Section A there is no choice; all students must do the same task. There is usually a substantial reading input (up to 400 words) which students need to assimilate and they are asked to produce one or more pieces of writing in response to it. About 250 words are required in total.

The task asks the student to do one or more of the following: apply the given information, select and summarise, elicit information or compare parts of the input. As the task is so well-defined and all students must do this part of the paper, credit can be given for specific features and appropriate expression.

In Section B there is a choice between four tasks. Each task fully describes the required response. The purpose of the writing and the intended audience will be stated in each case. The tasks vary from articles and reports to letters, instructions and expanded notes. Students are asked to produce about 250 words, as for Section A.

Sometimes the tasks appear in an appropriate format, such as an advertisement or a form. However, the reading load is much lighter in this section of the paper – about 60 words per task in total. In any one test there is a range of tasks and there is usually only one example of a particular type of writing.

If a particular form of response is required (e.g. a formal letter layout), this is indicated in the task.

Paper 3   English in Use

The English in Use paper is made up of three sections with about 75 questions in total. Each section carries equal weighting.

In Section A there are two modified cloze passages. In the first passage the gaps in the text emphasise mainly lexical points and the student is asked to select a word from four options. In the second passage, the gaps are selected to test structural elements of the language. There are no options here and students must decide on the best word according to their understanding of the text. Each passage has 15 gaps and is about 200 words long.

The cloze passages aim to test the student's knowledge of the formal elements of the language in context. From a testing point of view these exercises are useful, if somewhat inauthentic, because they can assess a wide range of lexical and structural features of the language. Both texts come from original sources such as newspapers or periodicals but may be modified in some way to make them more accessible for students at this level.

In Section B there are usually two exercises. In the first exercise the students are asked to recognise and correct errors or inappropriate features from a range including spelling, lexis, style, textual organisation and punctuation. The second exercise usually asks the student to adapt a text or to alter the style or register in some way to make it suitable for a particular purpose.

Both exercises are designed to test a student's ability to use the real-life skills of proof-reading or refining texts that could be required in study or at work. This section also encourages students to become aware of the need to correct and improve written work and enhance the skill of self-correction.

In Section C there are two exercises. One exercise usually asks the student to complete a gapped text with appropriate phrases. This is designed to assess the student's understanding of cohesion within sentences and between paragraphs. The other exercise will usually ask the student to expand notes into a fuller form. Here the aim is to test the student's manipulation of given elements. The students should be encouraged to be careful and accurate rather than creative or imaginative in this sort of question.

Although many of the texts used in this paper come from original sources, the lexical level is carefully controlled. Students are asked to transfer their answers on to OMR sheets as for Paper 1. Spaces allow for up to three-word answers. The last question is given appropriate space. Sample OMR sheets for Paper 3 are provided at the back of the Student's Book.

It is strongly recommended that students have plenty of practice with the OMR sheets so that they are not troubled by the mechanics of transferring their answers during the actual examination.

Paper 4   Listening

The Listening paper is recorded on audio tape, as in FCE and CPE, and all the time needed to read the questions, write the answers and transfer these to the OMR sheets is included on the tape. This is why the tape lasts longer than the same component for FCE or CPE. The actual test time is about 35 minutes, as for CPE. The Listening paper carries equal weighting (20 per cent) with the other papers and there are about 40 questions, using multiple choice, gap fill or matching techniques.

A sample OMR sheet for Paper 4 is provided at the back of the Student's Book.

It is strongly recommended that students have plenty of practice with the

Question aims and formats

OMR sheets so that they are not troubled by the mechanics of transferring their answers during the actual examination.

Sections A, C and D are heard twice and Section B *once only*. The delivery rate is at a normal accessible speed and light accents (American, Australian, etc.) are used when appropriate. In most cases the spoken texts are re-recorded with actors as it is difficult to control the linguistic features in authentic recordings. Some 'vox pop' pieces which are clear and of sufficient density for testing purposes may be used. Background noise may be used at the beginning of a recording in order to contextualise the extract but is faded out before the text is tested.

Questions normally follow the order of information in the text and, as in the Reading paper, questions which test overall understanding come towards the end of a set of questions.

The instructions on the question paper and the tape are the same and their aim is to establish a context for the listening passage as well as to give students clear guidance for answering the questions. Most of the questions only require one- or two-word answers or a brief phrase. The length of the gap should indicate the length of the answer required. Students should understand that writing full sentences is a waste of time.

Texts are based on the following types of listening material: radio broadcasts and announcements; conversations and discussions; speeches, talks and lectures; vox pop interviews.

In Section A there is a short text, usually a monologue, and students are asked questions which involve extracting specific information.

In Section B there is a short text which is heard once only. However, within the text there will be some repetition or re-phrasing. Students once again are required to extract information.

Section C is usually in the form of a dialogue or discussion and questions require an understanding of the gist or general impression, as well as the attitudes or points of view of the speakers.

Section D consists of a series of short extracts lasting about 10–30 seconds which are loosely linked by a theme. Questions test the student's ability to identify the speakers or source or the nature of the information they hear.

Paper 5 Speaking

The speaking test aims to produce a sample of language from students which includes both interactional and transactional language. It is divided into four phases in order to draw out these different types of language.

The language of interaction is that which occurs in initiating and maintaining social relations. The language may be imprecise and the participants tend to speak in short turns as the aim is to develop the relationship and participants need to balance their input.

Transactional language, however, aims to pass on information to listeners who in turn must respond in order to show that the message is understood. It is important for the structuring of the language to be clear and often the turns at speaking are longer than in an interactional situation.

Of course real-life language does not fall neatly into these categories but the oral interview aims to test both types of language, and for this reason the CAE always examines the students in pairs. There are also two examiners – an interlocutor and an assessor – and this helps to make this potentially subjective part of the examination more reliable.

Each part of the speaking test is designed to elicit either transactional or interactional language and it is the role of the interlocutor to guide the students through the tasks in order to produce an appropriate sample of their language.

The assessor, meanwhile, may concentrate on assessing the students according to the established criteria, although at the end of the test the assessor may participate in order to develop fully the interactive potential of the situation.

During any session the two examiners will exchange roles, but not during the examining of any one pair. The test will last 15 minutes.

The four phases of the speaking test are as follows:

Phase A In this part mainly social language is tested while the students introduce or are introduced to each other and answer direct questions from the interlocutor about their interests and activities, etc.

Phase B The interlocutor gives both students a visual prompt, such as a photograph or diagram. One of the students is asked to describe and comment on it in such a way as to help the other student see similarities and differences in their picture. The situation is then reversed and the other student is given a similar task. Transactional language is being tested here.

Phase C In this part both students are given the same problem-solving task and are given about three minutes to reach agreement or to exchange different points of view. This phase is testing the skills of negotiation and collaboration which involve both transactional and interactional language.
The tasks may fall into the categories of sequencing, ranking, comparing and contrasting.

Phase D In this section the assessor joins the group and may take the opportunity to redress any imbalance in the amount of language elicited from the students. This part of the test develops the issues raised in Phase C and allows all the participants to extend the views and ideas expressed. It is expected that the two students talk in short turns as directed by the examiner.
The aim of this phase is to allow the assessor and the interlocutor to 'fine-tune' their judgements and to refocus the interview if that has proved necessary.

Marking and grading

All five papers of the CAE examination carry equal weighting. Each of the five papers is marked out of a different total, but the scores are scaled by computer so that each paper contributes 20 per cent to the total mark.

Each paper is marked in a slightly different way. Samples of OMR sheets for Papers 1, 3 and 4 appear at the back of the Student's Book.

The Reading paper is marked by an optical mark reader (OMR). The OMR sheets are scanned by the reader which is programmed with the correct keys. Multiple choice and gapped text questions are worth 2 marks each. Multiple matching questions are worth 1 mark each.

The Writing paper is double-marked by EFL examiners who are trained and monitored through a co-ordination process. When necessary, third marking is carried out. A general table of descriptors and a task-specific mark-scheme for each question is used to enable examiners to award a mark out of 5 for each section, giving a raw mark out of 10 for the paper as a whole (see p. 18).

The English in Use paper is answered on OMR sheets which are then marked by trained markers using a carefully constructed mark-scheme. They are supervised by EFL examiners who monitor and moderate the marking process. The markers fill in the lozenge-shaped spaces for the correct mark to be awarded for each question. These are then fed into and read by the optical mark reader.

The Listening paper is marked in a similar way to the English in Use paper and the tightly controlled mark-scheme allows for a clerical marking process.

The Speaking paper is marked by two examiners, although only one mark is entered on the student's mark sheet. The mark is agreed between the two examiners. This OMR sheet is fed into the reader. See p. 21 for more detail.

The scores on the five components are added together by the computer after the correct weighting has been applied. The final 'aggregate' mark determines the student's grade.

The results slip

Each student receives a results slip which tells them what grade they have achieved. This is in the range from A through to E. A, B, and C are passing grades; D and E are failing grades.

Students who fail are given an indication of which papers were the weaker, while students who pass know which papers they did really well in. Very weak students receive an 'ungraded' result and this means they have performed very poorly in all components of the examination.

Assessment and marking of Paper 2 Writing

Paper 2 Writing – Sample answers

The following pieces of writing have been selected from students' answers produced during trialling. Marks have been awarded, based on the assessment criteria for the examination, in order to help teachers in assessing the work of their own students. Brief explanatory notes have been added to show how these marks were arrived at.

Sample answer A

Question answered: Practice Test 2 Section A
Mark: 5
Good range of language well-used. Task well covered. Intelligent use of stimulus.

a)
                                                           Winter Warmth
                                                           101, Green Street
                                                           Oakstead
                                                           OK2 4JH

                                                           23 September 1993

Robert J. Howlett
25-31 High Street
Oakstead
OK1 2AR

Dear Mr Howlett,

    I am writing on behalf of Winter Warmth, which is, as you possibly know, a local charity which supports homeless people. This association was founded in 1990 and has since then provided nightshelter and food for the many homeless people in this area.
    As you are known to be charitable and generous we would like to ask you for a donation. Your financial support would very much be appreciated with regard to the nightshelter which at the moment is still in the planning stage, but is expected to be open at the end of November. You can be assured that your money will be used only for this purpose and that it will be worked with carefully and efficiently. Your assistance would be a helpful contribution to our numerous volunteers, who are housewives, students etc.

Marking and grading

Please bear in mind that you help with this money people, who do not have any homes and who certainly will not survive the winter without the nightshelter of Winter Warmth.

I very much hope that we can count on your help.

Should you need any further information concerning our association, please do not hesitate to contact us.

I am looking forward to hearing from you.

Yours sincerely,
D. Hoffmann

b) Dear committee members and team leaders,

We would like to inform you that there will be a meeting on Monday at 6.30 in this office. The topics are a discussion about the letter to Mr. Howlett in which we ask for a donation, fund-raising in general and organising schedules.

Hope to see you all!
Yours Dagmar

Sample answer B

Question answered: Practice Test 1 Section B Question 2
Mark: 5
Few errors. Well organised, coherent, natural, appropriate, etc.

The Best Way to Study?

I started studying English at the age of 15 at a Commercial School in Switzerland. If I look back to it I realize that these studies were particularly based on grammar and written works, whereas conversation skills were neglected, thus the lessons were unfortunately very one-sided. In consequence, even after three years of English classes twice a week, I didn't feel confident enough to hold a general conversation in this language.

That's why I came to the conclusion that it is absolutely imperative to spend some time in an English-speaking country in order to learn to express myself fluently: There's no doubt in my mind that a major prerequisite for successful studies is that one is constantly surrounded by the foreign language. Therefore you should go to a place where you are virtually obliged to speak English. But in reality, it is rather difficult to find such a place, especially because study places which enjoy a good reputation are usually overcrowded with people who speak the same language than you do ... Therefore it is important, though sometimes very hard, to be selfrestricted enough not to take any other words in your mouth than English.

In my opinion, one of the best ways – and also one of the most pleasant – to practise understanding and improve vocabulary is to watch films and read books and newspapers. A nice method to improve spoken English and listening comprehension is certainly meeting native English speakers. It is pitty that this turns out to be somewhat difficult because, particularly in a town like Cambridge, a lot of people are not especially keen on becoming friends with foreign students. I appreciate their point to a certain extent since it might sometimes not be easy to make keen conversation with someone you hardly understand, at least in the beginning!

As to private lessons, I am confident that they are worth their money. I've never had the opportunity to ascertain myself of it but it seems logical to me that the less persons take part in a class the more each individual person must speak and concentrate. Obviously private lessons also enables a teacher to emphasise on a student's individual difficulties.

All things considered, I think that the time spent in a foreign country is an extremely precious experience.

Sample answer C

Question answered: Practice Test 1 Section A
Mark: 4
Register not always appropriate, but generally a good attempt at task with few errors.

a) Dear Sirs,

I write on behalf of The International Friendship Club to confirm the arrangement your travel agency has worked out for us.
15 of our members would like to see Macbeth on Saturday 16th of March.
As I am informed, the play starts at 8 pm and finishes at approximately 11 pm. Should there be any amendments in time or date, I should appreciate it if you would inform me as soon as possible. Owing to the fact that we are more than 10 persons we would like to call on your special offer of £6 per seat. This price will be paid on the night we arrive.
Should you need any further information do not hesitate to contact me.

Yours faithfully,
Dagmar Hoffmann

b) Dear Mr and Mrs Andersen,

Thank you for your letter of 21 January in which you expressed your dissatisfaction with the refusal of the English club to obtain tickets for your children for the visit to see Macbeth. Please allow me to give you an explanation for the decision of the Club. The Club is of the opinion that the story of Macbeth is too brutal for little ones. It is not a question of understanding English but of protecting your children of cruelty. I hope you understand and accept the club's decision. In this respect I would like to remind you of the great variety of kids' events that are offered in our club.

Marking and grading

I hope you will appreciate the club's point of view. Should you need any further assistance, do not hesitate to contact us.
  Yours sincerely,
  Dagmar Hoffman

c)   Dear Sam,

I executed the tasks you wrote on your last note. First of all I confirmed the details of our arrangement concerning the performance of Macbeth. Afterwards I wrote a letter to family Andersen explaining them the reasons why they cannot take their children to Macbeth.
  I am looking forward to hearing from you soon.

  Yours Dagmar

Sample answer D

Question answered: Practice Test 3 Section B Question 4
Mark: 4
A carefully planned and generally accurate attempt at task. Errors do not impede communication. Evidence of range of relevant language. Good attempt at suitable register.

THE DOS AND DONT's IN OUR COMPANY

WELCOME:
  First of all we welcome you to your own company, and hope that you will enjoy working with us as much as we are going to enjoy your company. To start working for this company here are some "Dos & Don'ts" which will help you to know the way we work.

The Dos:
  1. Always be punctual in coming to work, or in the time you take to finish the task you have.
  2. Work hard and accurately because we consider the quantity and quality of the work.
  3. Be cooperative with all you workmates so that your work finishes quickly.
  4. Tell us if you come across anything that you think needs to be attended to, so that your job is not delayed in anyway.
  5. We welcome any suggestions and queries you might think of or come across.
  6. If you need any help in your job ask the employees whom are not very busy.
  7. Report any faults or damages in the equipments or machinery you are using, and leave a label on them say "out of order".

8. Do leave your office as soon as possible when you hear the fire alarm by the nearest fire exit.
9. Do bring us any documents which prove you were in a sick leave.
10. Do enjoy you stay.

The Don'ts:
1. Don't hesitate to make friends in your firstday, and try to know everybody who you will work with from the first day.
2. Don't have any type of alcoholic drinks during your work time.
3. Don't forget to put all the equipments and lights off when you leave you office, and the keys after locking up every thing.
4. Don't leave todays work to tomorrow.
5. Dont smoke inside the premises.
6. Don't try to mend any equipments or machines yourself.
7. Don't park your car in others parking places.
8. Don't dress any type of dresss which are not suitable for the type of job you are doing.
9. Don't overwork.

Sample answer E

Question answered: Practice Test 1 Section B Question 3
Mark: 3
A reasonable attempt at the task, although a little short. Some good natural language but a number of basic errors.

February 26, 1993

Dear Mary:

Well, I hope that by this time you are already recovering. I think it was really a shame that you couldn't come with us. this holidays were fantastic but don't worry we've already planned our next holiday.

Any way, let me tell you what we did. As you now We had never been there before, so the experience was twice good. We rented a cottage near the river so we could cook our own meals. Very early in the morning we walked down the river, and during the day we did many diferent things like: swimming, sailing, hikking an so on. During the evinings we all sat in circle and make a fire and sang the tipical camping song. The last day of the trip we had a big B.B.Q. as the weather was wonderful.

Well, Mary onces againg it was a pity you couldn't come but there will be a next time. Ah, I will send you some of the picture we look, and I'm looking forward to meeting you and then tell you more about our plans for the next holidays.

With love.

Nelssy.

Marking and grading

Sample answer F

Question answered: Practice Test 1 Section B Question 5
Mark: 3
Reasonable attempt. The fruit farmers should at least consider employing him.

P J. R.
Avda. Moucayo, 101
Agreda,
SORIA. SPAIN

H. DAUNCE
Fullers Farm.
Little Cote, Nr Salisbury
Wilts. UK.

3 March, 1993.

Dear sir:

I write to you in connexion with your advertisement reqiuring help for your fruit . farm during July and August, as I am very interested in taking an this job.

I am an 18 years old student who lives in a rural area in Spain and who spends most of the time holding the last secunday school course and helping his parents with tasks they have to carry out as farmers. Therefore, picking, sorting and packing fruit are very familiar to me, as well as keeping house and garden in order.

Working for you those two months would be a priceless opportunity for me to improve the background of English., so useful as I intend to become a plane pilot; accordingly, lodge and modest wage you seem to offrer are sufficient in return for the effort I must put in.

On the other hand, I consider myself an easygoing healthy and cheerful young used to different atmospheres. since one of my hobbies is to travel all round the world every year.

In addition, I would like to inform you that, although. I got the licence no long ago, nevertheless, since then I have been driving a far distance from home to school every day, consequently, I have the skills your advertisement suggests.

Finally, I am glad to tell you that children are not an obstacle for me, on the contrary, I take to them. immediately.

I am looking. forward to hearing from you that this application has been successful

Yours sincerely
P. J. R.
student.

Marking and grading

Sample answer G

Question answered: Practice Test 4 Section A
Mark: 2
Serious misunderstanding of task leading to irrelevancies. Frequent basic errors.

a)
                                        911 Hills Road
                                        Cambridge
                                        CB2 2QT

Royal Bridge Hotel   4th March 1993
Merrinmouth

Dear Sir/Madam,
    I am writing to complain about the fact that my family and I, who spent some days in your Hotel last week, have found it completly different from your brochure's description.
    First of all the accomodation neither was located on an exciting view of the sunny Merrimouth's Bay, nor was elegant as you said (promised). The same for the restaurant that was always overcrowded and situated on a steep hill above a main road so noisy and unconfortable.
    Unfortunatly also the sport facilities were different from what we'll expected: the Stingo's Health Club was a cramped basament, the 18-hole course at Gruham Hall was closed down and amy way miles away from the Hotel, the hot air balooning was ridiculously expenlive and worst of all the pool was closed for a couple of days for safety checks
    Last but not least the entertainment offered were really pathetic and of a bad quality, infact: we had got vulgar comedy shows, a terribly noise disco always playing music completly out of fashion and my husband and I couldn't have had our dreamed romantic nights because the children's hostess, owing to illness, was not available during last weekend.
    For all these reasons I would like to have a reduction on my fees otherwise I will sue you for damage. (?!

    Yours faithfully
    Mari Claudia

b)
                                          911 Hills Road
                                        Cambridge
                                        CB2 2QT

                                        March 7th

Dear Marc,
    I hope you and the family are well.

Marking and grading

I am writing to apologise about all the problems we're had got during our holiday two weeks ago at the "   ".

I've been really disappointed about the Hotel's facilities we "haven't had" there; but, belive me, it was completly different from the brochure I saw before deciding for it.

But, don't worry, yesterday I posted a complain letter to Mr Fox (Do you remember the Hotel Manager?) in which I explain everythink (all the things that) went wrong when we were there and I asked them to have a reduction in our fees.

So, as soon as it's possible I'm going to write you their answer and eventually I'll provide to let you have your ammount of money.
Wait from me soon.

Best wishes
Claudia

Sample answer H

Question answered: Practice Test 3 Section B Question 2
Mark: 2
Numerous errors impede communication. Some attempt at organisation but not very coherent. Register and relevance shaky.

OUR SCHOOL IN THE FILM

last Wednesday, we had a very famous visitor who works as a singer in Japan. Although Japanese students know, of course, the other student never know. I am afraid.

Now I will tell you about her. Her name is Seiko Matsuda. She was most popular singer in our generation and even now I have never seen such an attract singer. Moreover all her songs had been brought incredible sensation for ages therefore they had always showed the best hit chart. However she got married with a famous actor who is called Masaki Honda about five years ago. After marriage, her image which was in our mind completely changed. more mysterious and attractive ….

Incidentally this her visit was for taking a film. She apparently performed as a teacher in a language school. The reason which she and the film staff chose our school was considered the most beautiful and wonderful school in England. How brilliant! When we talked to her, she also said that our school was really nice and she had wanted to study like our school. In fact she studied English in America.

As a result, we are the happiest student who is studying in the wonderful school. Don't you think so? We are very proud of our school. As you might know. Japanese English education system has slightly mistaked. The film will be showed against such a wrong education. We do hope that it will change as soon as possible. People who showed the film will recognized that English is important and very difficult to master. They can also see the diffrence culture between Japanese and European.

On the other hand Japanese will be able to recognize our original culture and we will love their country more than before.

Of course we also recommended the film to you. You can understand about Japan and Japanese people. Fortunately the film will be sent after finishing to take it. Don't worry it is spoken in English

Sample answer I

Question answered: Practice Test 4 Section B Question 4
Mark: 1
Language elementary with frequent basic errors. Too short, so poor coverage of task.

My flat was built about 10 years ago and is located by the main road. It has 5 bedrooms, 2 bathrooms, kitchem, dimimg room, sitting room, amd balcomy.

<u>bedrooms & bathrooms</u>
This flat has ome bedroom fitted with a bathroom. This room is the biggest in this flat and the others are a little smaller tham this.

<u>kitchem & dinimg room</u>
Kitchem has a high-rate, huge refrigerator, a room for storimg food, a simk, a overn, amd cupboard. Dimimg room is located just by the kitchem amd you cam watch T.V. while you are havimg meal. Because the sitting room is mext to the dimimg room.

<u>Sitting room</u>
It particularly has a T.V. whose screen is 25" big, and also it has a mice coach.

<u>balcomy</u>
There are a lot of kimds of plamts in the balcomy, you cam dry your wet clothes.

Mamy supermarkets. restauramts, chemistry etc is all in 5 minutes walkimg. Futhermore, the bus stop is just in fromt of this flat, so you cam easily use a public tramsport.

Marking and grading

Paper 2 Writing – Assessment criteria

This table shows the typical features of work gaining each mark. These include quality of language (i.e. grammar, lexis, spelling, punctuation, syntax) and task achievement (i.e. content, organisation, relevance, completeness, cohesion, style, register).

5	Very positive effect on target reader. Minimal errors. Resourceful, controlled and natural use of language showing a good range of vocabulary and structure. Completion of task: well-organised, good use of cohesive devices, appropriate register, no relevant omissions. N.B. Not necessarily absolutely flawless!
4	Sufficiently natural, errors only when more complex language attempted. Some evidence of range of vocabulary and structure. A good attempt at achieving the task. Any omissions are only minor. Attention paid to organisation and cohesion; register not always natural but positive effect on target reader achieved.

3	Either: Reasonable attempt at task and language, but little variety.
	     or: Original task and language with errors which do not impede communication.
	     or: Unadventurous but fairly accurate task and language. Possibly poorly adapted lifting in Section A.
	No significant irrelevancies or omissions.

2	Errors sometimes obscure communication and/or language too elementary. Some attempt at task but notable omissions and/or lack of organisation and cohesion would have negative effect on reader.
1	Serious lack of control and/or frequent basic errors. Narrow range of language. Inadequate attempt at task.

0	Either: Fewer than 50 words per question.
	     or: Totally illegible.
	     or: Totally irrelevant.

Notes

Legibility: Students should be warned that they will lose marks if their work is very difficult to read.

Length: Answers which are either much shorter or much longer than the recommended 250 words will not be penalised, but students should be aware that short answers are likely to lose marks for omissions and over-long ones for irrelevancy.

Spelling: Poor spelling is penalised if it interferes with communication. American spelling is accepted provided it is consistent.

Assessment and marking of Paper 5 Speaking

Criteria

There are five criteria for assessment. The brief descriptors on the grid should be read in conjunction with the notes given below.

Fluency

This relates to the naturalness of the speed and rhythm, together with the lack of hesitations and pauses. Pauses to marshal thoughts rather than language are regarded as natural features of spoken interaction and not penalised.

Accuracy

This refers to the range (quantity) and correctness (quality) of both grammatical structures and vocabulary. Major errors (i.e. those which obscure the message) are penalised more heavily than minor ones (i.e. those which do not obscure the message). Obvious or self-corrected slips of the tongue are not penalised.

Pronunciation

This covers both individual sounds and prosodic or utterance-level features such as stress-timing, rhythm, placing of stress, intonation patterns, and range of pitch within utterances. Candidates' pronunciation is not expected to be entirely free of L1 features, even at band 8.

Task achievement

This scale refers to candidates' participation in the four phases of the Speaking paper and covers the following areas:

- fullness of candidate's contributions
- appropriacy or relevance of contributions to the tasks
- independence in carrying out the tasks set (i.e. the degree to which candidates can carry out the tasks without prompting or redirection by the interlocutor or the other candidate)
- the organisation of the candidate's contributions (logical or coherent sequencing of utterances)
- a candidate's flexibility or resourcefulness
- the degree to which a candidate's language contributes to successful task management through the selection of appropriate language functions and vocabulary.

The attempt to complete the tasks is what is being assessed; failure to reach a 'right' or complete answer within the time available is not penalised.

Interactive communication

This refers to a candidate's ability to interact both actively and responsively, and includes the candidate's sensitivity to the norms of turn-taking appropriate

Marking and grading

to each phase of the paper. Aggression, deliberate dominance or intimidation is penalised; a candidate whose partner behaves in such a way is not penalised. Candidates who are unwilling or unable to take their turns adequately will receive a reduced score on this scale.

The mark bands

Teachers may find it helpful to compare the CAE Paper 5 mark bands with the standards expected at CPE and FCE.

7–8 band Candidates scoring 7 or 8 would probably also be capable of passing CPE.
5–6 band Very good FCE candidates might achieve such marks, at their very best.
3–4 band A narrow fail at CAE, but probably a pass at FCE.
1–2 band A clear fail at CAE and probably at FCE too.

Paper 5 Speaking – Assessment criteria

This table shows the typical oral features gaining these marks.

	Fluency	Accuracy	Pronunciation	Task achievement	Interactive communication
7–8	Coherent spoken interaction with appropriate speed. Few intrusive hesitations.	Evidence of a wide range of structures and vocabulary. Errors minimal in number and gravity.	Little L1 accent/ L1 accent not intrusive. Good mastery of English pronunciation features.	The tasks are dealt with fully and effectively, with notable coherence and organisation of salient points. The language is fully appropriate to each task.	Contributes fully and effectively throughout the interaction, with sensitivity to the inorms of turn-taking in each task.
5–6	Occasional but noticeable hesitations, but not such as to strain the listener or impede communication. Pauses to marshall ideas rather than language.	Evidence of a good range of structures and vocabulary; has the range needed to express intention. Number and gravity of errors do not impede communication.	Noticeable L1 accent having minor difficulties with some pronunciation features. These rarely strain the listener and do not impede communication.	The tasks are dealt with effectively but treatment may be fragmented or a little unsystematic. The language is generally appropriate with only isolated lapses.	Contributes with ease for most of the interaction, with only occasional and minor difficulties in negotiation or turn-taking.
3–4	Fairly frequent and noticeable hesitations. Communication is achieved but strains the listener at times. May pause to marshall language.	Fairly frequent errors and evidence that limited range of structures and vocabulary restrict ability to express intent. These do not prevent communication of the essential message.	Obvious L1 pronunciation features with major defects. These may frequently strain the listener and/or make comprehension of detail difficult.	One or more of the tasks dealt with in a limited manner. Language is noticeably inappropriate at several points. Redirection may be required at times.	Contributes effectively for some of the interaction, but with intrusive difficulties or deviations at times. Responses may be short without attempt at elaboration.
1–2	Disconnected speech and/or frequent hesitations impede communication and constantly strain the listener.	Frequent basic errors and limited range of structures and/or vocabulary impede communication of the essential message and constantly strain the listener.	Heavy L1 pronunciation and widespread difficulties with English features impede communication of the message and constantly strain the listener.	Inadequate or irrelevant attempts at the tasks using little appropriate language. Requires major or repeated redirection or assistance with tasks.	Difficulty in maintaining contributions throughout. May respond to simple or structured interaction but obvious imitations in freer circumstances.
0	Sample of language inadequate for assessment (even after prompting by the interlocutor).				

Preparing students for CAE

Paper 1 Reading

Many students will initially find the high reading load for this paper very daunting. It is important therefore that careful, step-by-step preparation is employed to bring them to the stage where they can confidently tackle a whole paper in one hour.

Before focusing on reading at speed, ensure that students are equipped to extract information from all aspects of a text. If practicable, familiarise them with a variety of printed materials: guidebooks, textbooks, periodicals, brochures, newspapers, etc. If this is difficult, use EFL sources which present authentic reading texts in their original layout. Teach your students to observe headlines, typeface, page layout, punctuation, etc. as a guide to provenance and register *before* reading, and to observe lexical and structural clues *while* they read.

Draw students' attention to the variety of question types used and encourage them to use the question format as a guide to the *type* of reading skill being tested. For example, questions preceding the text often indicate that the text should be scanned for specific information. It is a waste of time to plod through every last word (e.g. Practice Test 1, Paper 1, First text).

Some multiple-matching exercises (e.g. Practice Test 2, Paper 1, First text) on the other hand, may require close reading of the text. It will often be useful for students to underline the relevant parts of the text (e.g. Practice Test 2, Paper 1, Fourth text, the *names* listed A–H), during the first read through, to save time searching while they complete the matching exercise. Multiple-matching exercises lend themselves particularly well to pair or group work, as a basis for discussion, and it is advisable to give students several practice sessions in a relaxed classroom context so that they are not disconcerted by having to do such an exercise alone for the first time.

Paragraph gapping (e.g. Practice Test 1, Paper 1, Third text) is a test of students' understanding of the text as a whole, its structure and coherence. Advise students to read the gapped text, skipping the gaps, to form a general idea of how it develops. Train them to observe internal signs (such as use of pronouns, sequencing adverbials) to check how the given paragraphs fit, in addition to judging by their content. This type of exercise can be prepared for by students in small groups: they write straightforward narratives of five short paragraphs. They copy paragraphs 1, 3 and 5 on to another paper and hand it to a classmate. The other student must fill the gaps with invented paragraphs. These can be compared with the originals. Alternatively, the narrative may be cut into paragraphs and a traditional sequencing exercise carried out.

Paper 2   Writing

The writing tasks which students are set in this paper are always contextualised. The students therefore know not only *what* they must write (e.g. a letter, a report), but also for *whom* they are writing, and *why*. This releases both students and teachers from having to practise 'essays' which serve no purpose other than demonstrating command of formal writing conventions. However, contextualisation of tasks means that students must be able to gauge the style and register appropriate to a range of situations and produce suitable written work. Learning to judge how to write, as well as what to write, can usefully be linked to work for the Reading paper, although the level of language which students are expected to produce is not, of course, the same as that which they should be able to understand.

Section A

This compulsory exercise is designed to allow students maximum scope to demonstrate their ability to express themselves in writing, by providing all the necessary information. Two ground rules must be observed in practising this type of task. First, the information must not be altered, although it may be added to; second, some information will probably have to be ignored, as irrelevant to the given task. Students should be advised first of all to spend adequate time on analysing the task so that they are absolutely clear about what they have to do. They should then mark up the text, picking out essential information and making connections where relevant. It will usually be a good idea to sketch a brief sequential plan as well, incorporating any additional ideas of their own. This will enable them to concentrate on the accuracy and appropriacy of their language as they write. It will be very useful, and productive, to take students through the three preparatory stages, outlined above, in class, before they settle to write on their own. The preparation can be done first of all as a teacher-led activity, then by students working in groups or in pairs, as they become more confident.

Section B

In this section, students must draw largely on their own imagination, experience, or knowledge. As in Section A, it is important that careful analysis of the task is undertaken in order to pinpoint the purpose and context of the writing. Otherwise students may produce work which, although interesting and accurate, is marked down because it is inappropriate. This is especially true of some tasks which *appear* very simple. For example, in Practice Test 3, Paper 2, Section B, Question 2, students may feel certain that they can invent a story about their favourite rock star. However, the task sets out the information required and students who fail to suit their answer to this would certainly lose marks. The temptation to 'bend' the task must be resisted. Sometimes an apparently more challenging task will in fact turn out to be quite straightforward.

   It should be noted that Section B does not normally contain a question which requires the same form and register as Section A. That is, if Section A requires an informal letter, there will not usually be one in Section B; if

Section A requires a report, there will not usually be one in Section B, and so on. Students must be prepared to write both formal and informal language.

Paper 3   English in Use

Section A

The two modified cloze exercises in this section can be approached in different ways. It will help students to spend class time developing an appropriate pattern for each. These could be:

1. *Lexical cloze*
   Step 1: Read through text quickly to get overall picture.
   Step 2: Answer item by item, using contextual clues where appropriate.

2. *Structural cloze*
   Step 1: Read through (as above).
   Step 2: *Attempt* to fill gaps, checking context *before and after* for clues.
   Point out that: (a) gaps are sometimes interdependent, e.g. ... *so* small *that* ... ;
   (b) if stuck, they should ignore gap and go on – it may be easier when the text is more or less complete.

N.B. For both cloze exercises, students should remember *never* to leave blanks, however uncertain they are. Guesses *can* be right, blanks cannot!

Section B

The skills tested in both parts of Section B can be practised in teaching exercises which may form part of the class routine.

3. *Error correction*
   Students should be encouraged to check their own, or colleagues', work. Checking for specific types of error can be integrated with study of particular aspects of language, for example, spelling (Practice Test 1, Paper 3, Question 3).

4. *Amending style or register*
   Students may be asked to write informal notes on a given subject and then to exchange texts and amend each other's notes. This kind of exercise can form a useful introduction to considerations of the language used in different contexts, which is also relevant to the Writing paper.

Section C

These exercises may be used in lessons where students are studying the structure of language, especially at clause level.

5. *Text completion*
   Students should be encouraged to observe and employ the variety of devices which link and order a text. It is usually best to begin practice at a basic level, joining simple clauses to form complex sentences, using relative pronouns and so on.

6. *Expansion*
   This kind of exercise can be used to practise structural accuracy, for example when studying the formation and sequencing of tenses, word order (e.g. adjectives and adverbials), or the use of articles and other determiners.

Paper 4 Listening

For this paper, students need both dedicated practice to learn specific listening strategies and exposure to as much and as varied spoken language as possible. For students not in an English-speaking environment, this exposure may be very difficult to achieve. Students should be given every encouragement to listen to English outside the classroom (see suggestions in Student's Book, pages vii–viii).

As far as technique is concerned, familiarity with the formats in these practice tests and careful attention to rubrics will enable students to concentrate on the meanings and implications relevant to individual tasks. Encourage students to use the time before they hear the texts wisely. They should try to predict the topic and use the questions as prompts while listening. They should also be reassured that although they must spell correctly, the words they must write will all be familiar ones, or easily guessable.

Section A is normally a straightforward information text, heard twice. The questions often offer helpful clues about the text, and students should be aware of this.

Section B may need more practice as it is heard only once. Students should learn to listen for the repetitions *within* the text.

Section C may be linked to oral practice. The speaker(s) will generally be expressing feelings and attitudes rather than giving information. Stress and intonation exercises may be based on sections of text, or used as a lead-in to the listening work.

Section D can often be presented as a class exercise. For example, before hearing the rubric, the class can be asked to guess the theme. Afterwards students can be asked to choose one speaker and develop the utterance further in mini role-playing exercises.

Paper 5 Speaking

Because speaking skills are tested with pairs of candidates, it is relatively easy to incorporate examination practice into class activities. Specific exam preparation need cover little more than an explanation of the four phases (see page 7, and materials for the Speaking paper within each test). The social, interactional and transactional language required can be practised in the pair-work phase of oral lessons, using the visual prompts provided. This can also form the basis of valuable writing exercises, as follow-up work. For example, after using the picture of food in Practice Test 1 for oral pair work, there could be some revision of structures used to make suggestions followed by a class discussion on healthy eating or food fashions, with written homework in the form of a letter of advice.

Practice Test 1

Paper 1 Reading (1 hour + 15 minutes)

First text: 1 E   2 J (1 and 2 interchangeable)
               3 F   4 G   5 I (3, 4 and 5 interchangeable)
               6 H   7 I   8 G   9 A   10 C   11 B   12 D
               13 G   14 D   15 J   16 B   17 C   18 E   19 F

Second text: 20 B   21 D   22 A   23 D   24 C   25 C

Third text: 26 E   27 A   28 D   29 G   30 C   31 F

Fourth text: 32 F
               33 B   34 F   35 G (33, 34 and 35 interchangeable)
               36 C   37 C   38 D   39 E   40 A   41 F   42 H
               43 D   44 F   45 A

Paper 2 Writing (2 hours)

See pages 9–18 for assessment criteria and sample answers.

Paper 3 English in Use (1 hour 30 minutes)

Section A

Question 1 [One mark for each correct answer]

1 A   2 B   3 C   4 D   5 A   6 B   7 C   8 D   9 A
10 A   11 B   12 C   13 D   14 A   15 C

Question 2 [One mark for each correct answer]

16 are   17 in/when/before   18 is   19 Otherwise   20 the
21 this/so 22 substitute/replacement   23 with   24 else   25 itself
26 not   27 that/this   28 it   29 can/may   30 or

Practice Test 1

Section B

Question 3 [One mark for each correct answer]

31 Principle 32 √ 33 distinction 34 √ 35 exciting
36 pieces 37 √ 38 Experience 39 development 40 further
41 indivisible 42 already 43 research 44 behaviour

Question 4 [One mark for each correct answer]

45 must/should inform 46 later than 47 only 48 satisfied
49 regard/reference/respect 50 following 51 punctual
52 compulsory 53 completion 54 conditions 55 full
56 written 57 circumstances 58 recommendation

Section C

Question 5 [One mark for each correct answer]

59 G 60 J 61 A 62 D 63 C 64 K 65 I

Question 6 [These are specimen answers – up to two marks for each sentence]

81 A hire car has been booked from Bristows, the garage opposite the station, for which a £25 deposit is payable on collection.
82 From Bristows turn left into Station Road, then follow the Coast Road, which is clearly signed, for 3 km until you reach Ocean Ridge cottage at the top of the hill.
83 The water supply is already connected, but for electricity you need some £1 coins to put in the meter, which is behind the door.
84 The phone in the hall accepts incoming calls only.
85 Please remember to supervise children whenever they use the path from the back garden to the beach as it is very steep, and the cottage owner cannot be held responsible for accidents.
86 Always lock the cottage when you go out because unfortunately there have been frequent thefts from holiday homes recently, resulting in the loss of valuables such as cash, credit cards and cameras.

Paper 4 Listening (45 minutes)

Section A [One mark for each correct answer]

1 famous 2 national 3 origins (and development)
4 (the) Middle Ages 5 (early) industrial machines 6 living conditions
7 Living Memories 8 prints/works

Section B [One mark for each correct answer]

9 National Zoological Society 10 Maria Altrim 11 Open Partnerships

Practice Test 1

12 Forward Thinking   13 Eastern Land Conservation   14 D(octo)r Scott   15 Land Chemistry   16 Harnessing the Wind

Section C [One mark for each correct answer]
17 J   18 KJ   19 J   20 K   21 N   22 K   23 K   24 J

Section D [One mark for each correct answer]
25 B   26 A   27 G   28 F   29 E   30 E   31 G   32 A
33 C   34 H

Transcript

This is the Certificate in Advanced English, Listening Test. Practice Test number 1. There are four sections to the test, A, B, C and D. You will hear Section B once only. All the other parts of the test will be heard twice. During the test, there will be a pause before each part to allow you to look through the questions, and other pauses to let you think about your answers. At the end of every pause you will hear this sound.

tone

You should write your answers on the question paper. You will have ten minutes at the end to transfer your answers to the separate answer sheet. The tape will now be stopped. You must ask any questions now, as you will not be allowed to speak during the test.

[pause]

Section A. You will hear a museum guide welcoming a party of visitors. Look at the notes below and complete the information for questions 1–8 using up to three words in each space. You will hear the recording twice.

[pause]

tone

Guide: Good morning everyone and welcome to Lampley and District Museum. Before you go round, I'd just like to tell you a little about how the museum is organised. It was founded twenty-five years ago, and brings together under one roof the contents of the former Lampley Guild Hall collection and the South Welting Gallery. Since its foundation it has received a number of bequests, and also gifts from the local archaeological society. The collection is divided into four sections.

First of all, we attempt to put Lampley on the national map, so to speak, with our collection of portraits illustrating some of the city's more famous sons and daughters. There is also, currently, a montage of pictures, photographs and documents concerned with events of national significance, seen in the lives of the people of Lampley.

Having, we hope, whetted your appetites, we then take a longer view of the city. In Section Two, we have first of all a series of maps and cases of exhibits related to the origins and early development of the city, and then next, these lead us into some displays, which are in fact reconstructions and are the work of a local school, and are both extraordinarily detailed and accurate, illustrating life in Lampley in the Middle Ages. I'm sure you will be fascinated by them.

Section Three will be of interest to any of you who like machines, as well as social historians. After a period of relative obscurity, Lampley grew vigorously during the Industrial Revolution, and we have several working models of early machines used in the region's factories. Of course, in the early days, there was a great influx of workers and their families, and although we in Lampley have always prided ourselves on the generally enlightened attitudes of the industrialists in the area, the images in the last part of Section Three does remind us that living conditions were pretty dreadful for industrial workers a hundred and fifty years ago. In Section Four, we have again drawn on the resources of our younger citizens, who have been guided for several years past by our curator in the putting together of a regularly up-dated audio-visual exhibition based entirely on reminiscences and eye-witness accounts of local and national events. It's entitled 'Living Memories' and it's very popular with both old and young visitors.

Lastly, also in Section Four, we have a small collection of works by some of the best artists currently working in the region. With our limited space, we can't represent them all together, so exhibits are renewed monthly. At present Lampley Contemporary Printmakers are having a show, and all the works are for sale. Now I hope you'll enjoy going round the museum and please don't hesitate to ask me if you have any questions. I'll do my best to answer them! Thank you.

[*pause*]

tone

Now you will hear the piece again. [The recording is repeated.]

[*pause*]

That is the end of Section A.

[*pause*]

Section B. You will hear a recording from the telephone answering machine of a conference organiser. As you listen, fill in the information on the booking forms for questions 9–16. Listen very carefully as you will hear this piece only once.

[*pause*]

tone

Answering machine: Thank you for calling the International Conference Centre. This line is for the registration of options at the next conference. If you have any queries please call the information line number in your brochure. To register for options, please leave a message on this line now, stating clearly the name of your organisation, your name, and the options chosen, which should be two in number. Please begin after the tone.

Caller 1: This is ... the National Zoological Society, erm Zoological Society, erm, I am Maria Altrim, That's A-L-T-R-I-M, that's M

Practice Test 1

	for mother, Altrim, erm and we would like to register for two optional sessions, erm, first, the one called 'Open Partnerships' which is in the morning, and then after lunch we'd like, erm, to join the discussion group called, erm, 'Forward Thinking'. Erm, that's all.
Caller 2:	My name's – oh sorry, my organisation is Eastern – Land – Conservation. And my name is Doctor Scott, that's Scott with a double T, and, er, we'd like to enrol for the sessions called 'Land Chemistry' and 'Harnessing the Wind'. That's 'Land Chemistry' in the morning, and 'Harnessing the Wind' in the afternoon. Um, er, thank you.

[*pause*]

That is the end of Section B.

[*pause*]

Section C. You will hear a radio programme in which a mother, Jane, and a father, Kenneth, discuss whether it is a good idea for young people to take a year out before going to university, to travel around the world. During their discussion they express various views. For questions 17–24, indicate which views are expressed by Jane and Kenneth, by writing J (for Jane) or K (for Kenneth) or N (for neither) in the box provided. You may write both initials if Jane and Kenneth express the same opinion. You will hear the piece twice.

[*pause*]

tone

Kenneth:	... the thing is, as I see it, it's really an opportunity they shouldn't waste, I mean, it's a privilege, even in affluent countries ...
Jane:	Well, yes, of course, I'm not saying that university isn't important, it's the age that isn't so crucial, I think. It doesn't matter really whether you're twenty-one or twenty-three or even thirty, a university degree is a university degree, but the chance to go all over the place, to see other countries, other cultures, before you're set in your ways, without a lot of preconceived ideas, prejudices even ...
Kenneth:	Mm, well ...
Jane:	I think that's what we should see this as. And meeting people.
Kenneth:	I don't deny it's good to have friends all round the world, and of course, the younger you are, the easier you make them, you're less inhibited ...
Jane:	Well, exactly, it's ideal. And you can afford to be adventurous because you know there's somewhere you can retreat to, somewhere you can run and hide, in your parents' place.
Kenneth:	I don't know about that.
Jane:	Oh, surely?
Kenneth:	I'm not so sure. But I do think, provided they're sensible in what they do, the experience, the knowledge of the world, that's going to stand them in good stead when it comes to prospective employers. They're going to be sounding as if they know a thing or two, give them the edge over the others in the office. That's where the outlay is going to be justified because, well, after all, it's going to cost a bob or two, isn't it?

Jane:	Well, it would if they wanted to do it in luxury, but that's the point, when they're young they can rough it a bit without minding, so they can do it on a tight budget.
Kenneth:	I still think I, we, whoever, we're going to end up well out of pocket. You just have to hope it's a worthwhile investment. So, although they may be late starters, have got a bit of catching up to do, career-wise, the boss'll be so taken with their maturity of approach, he …
Jane:	Or she …
Kenneth:	True. Or she, will value them anyway.
Jane:	They should learn to use their common sense, if nothing else.
Kenneth:	Personally, I think that's something you're born with. No amount of travel, however old or young you are, will give you that!
Jane:	Do you really? Well, it's a point of view, I suppose…

[*pause*]

tone

Now you will hear the piece again. [The recording is repeated.]

[*pause*]

That is the end of Section C.

[*pause*]

Now look at Section D for the fourth and last part of the test. You will hear extracts of five different people talking. They are all talking about some kind of meeting. Look at Task One. Letters A–H list various different people. As you listen, put them in order by completing the boxes numbered 25–29 with the appropriate letter. Now look at Task Two. Letters A–H list the different meetings mentioned by the people speaking in the extracts. As you listen, put them in order by completing the boxes numbered 30–34 with the appropriate letter. You will hear the series twice.

[*pause*]

tone

Businessman:	Well, I said, I told him, you can't honestly expect me to go through the whole deal here. It was a real hole. Anyway, they soon realised they'd misjudged their man, and sent a limo to whisk me out to company HQ. And I got the red carpet treatment there, no mistake. Met the chairman and the board, and had lunch with them! There's great potential there if we make a quick follow-up.
Mother:	You'll have to explain yourself to Dad. You're old enough to make your own apologies. Do you know he waited three-quarters of an hour for you at the bus station, in case you were on the next one. I can tell you he's not at all amused.
Local government official:	Now, that's an example of what makes this worthwhile. I've just been round to the hospital, and talked to the

Practice Test 1

	contractor. He's a decent chap, like I said, and, er, he saw our point of view. We can't waste taxpayers' money, I said, and he said, fair enough and he'll have the revised documents here by Monday.
Former schoolfriend:	It was that new place out near the station, you know? I'd have known her anywhere. There she was, the last person in the world you'd think of running a restaurant. She always came bottom in domestic science! Wouldn't have missed it for the world. Spent much longer than I'd planned of course, but, what the hell, it was such a coincidence. There was so much to catch up on.
Rock star:	Somehow I'd thought they'd be different. You get so many idiots, following whatever the papers tell them, you know, whoever's flavour of the month. Well, these guys had been so, I don't know, loyal, whatever, I thought, they'll understand what I'm trying to say to audiences, they'll have thought about what the words mean, you know. But they're just like all the others, it's the glamour that attracts them.

[*pause*]

tone

Now you will hear the piece again. [The recording is repeated.]

[*pause*]

That is the end of Section D. There will now be a ten-minute pause for you to transfer your answers to the separate answer sheet. Be sure to follow the numbering of all the questions. The question papers and answer sheets will then be collected by your supervisor.

[*pause*]

That is the end of the test.

Paper 5 Speaking   (15 minutes)

Note: In the examination, there will be both an assessor and an interlocutor in the room. The following notes use plural forms where appropriate, although we realise a teacher may often be working alone for practice sessions.
You will need to refer to Paper 5 of Practice Test 1 in the Student's Book and the colour section 'Visual materials for Paper 5' also in the Student's Book.

Phase A   (approximately three minutes)

INTRODUCTIONS

Good morning. My name is ... and this is my colleague ...
And your names are?
First of all we'd like to know a little about you. Do you know each other?

Practice Test 1

If yes:
> In that case, perhaps you (*Candidate A*) would like to tell us a little about (*Candidate B*) – where (s)he's from, what his/her hobbies and interests are, what (s)he does, *etc.*
> And (*Candidate B*), would you like to introduce us to (*Candidate A*) now, please?
> How long have you known each other?
> (*If applicable:*)
> What do you know about each other's country?

If no:
> Could you please find out about each other? Ask each other where you're from, what you're interested in, how you like to spend your time, why you're learning English, your plans for the future, your families, what you do, *etc.* (*select as applicable*)

GENERAL SOCIAL CONVERSATION

If in UK:
> (*Candidate A*), could you tell (*Candidate B*) what it's like to live in …
> (*Candidate B*), do you think you would like to visit …?
> (*Candidate B*), could you now tell (*Candidate A*) about where you live?
> How long are you staying here?
> Both of you come from places that are rather different from England. What do you think are the biggest differences?
> Is there anything in particular that you like or dislike about England? *etc.*

In candidates' country:
> Well, you both live here in … What would you say are the good things about living in …? Are there any disadvantages?
> How do you get to school/work?
> What is the best way of travelling round here? *etc.*

Phase B   (three or four minutes)

1   PONDS (Describe and identify)

> In this part of the test I'm going to give each of you some pictures to look at. Please do not show your pictures to each other.
> *Indicate pond pictures 1A–1F to Candidate A and pond pictures 1G–1M to Candidate B.*
> You each have pictures of the same six ponds but your pictures are in a different order.
> (*Candidate A*), I'd like you to choose one of the pictures and describe it to (*Candidate B*). You have about one minute to do this.
> (*Candidate B*), I'd like you to listen and then decide which picture is being described. If you are still uncertain after (*Candidate A*) has finished, you may ask him/her questions to help you identify the picture. Otherwise, say briefly what helped you recognise the picture.

Practice Test 1

All right? So, (*Candidate A*), would you start please?
(*Candidate A speaks for approximately one minute.*)
Thank you. Now, (*Candidate B*), have you spotted which pond it is?
(*Candidate B speaks for approximately 20 seconds.*)
Thank you very much. Now, would you like to compare your pictures?

2 | STATIONS (Compare and contrast) |

Now I'm going to give each of you a picture to look at. Please do not show your pictures to each other.
Indicate railway station picture 1N to Candidate B and railway station picture 1P to Candidate A.
Your pictures are similar but not the same. I'd like you, (*Candidate B*), to describe your picture fully to (*Candidate A*). You have about one minute to do this. I'd like you, (*Candidate A*), to listen carefully and then tell us very briefly two things which are the same as and two things which are different from (*Candidate B*)'s picture.
(*Candidate A*), here is some paper if you want to make any notes. Do you understand? So, would you like to begin please (*Candidate B*)?
(*Candidate B speaks for approximately one minute.*)
Thank you. Now, (*Candidate A*), I'd like you to tell (*Candidate B*) briefly how your picture is the same as and different from his/hers.
(*Candidate A speaks for approximately 20 seconds.*)
Thank you very much. Now, would you like to compare your pictures?

Phase C   (three or four minutes)

| A BALANCED DIET (Evaluate and rank order) |

Indicate food picture 1Q to the pair of candidates.
Here is a picture of food. I'd like you to talk about the different kinds of food and discuss which three are important elements of a balanced diet, and which three are the least important and say why. Which of them do you yourselves eat? Can you think of other essential foods?
You have three or four minutes for this.

Phase D   (three or four minutes)

Which did you agree were the most important?
Why is it important to think carefully about eating a balanced diet?
Do you sometimes eat things which aren't very good for you? Does it matter?
Which is the most important meal of the day? Why?
Do you think there are fashions in food? For example …?
How do you think eating habits will change in the future?

Practice Test 2

Paper 1 Reading (1 hour + 15 minutes)

First text:
1 B   2 D   3 A   (1, 2 and 3 interchangeable)
4 J   5 G   (4 and 5 interchangeable)
6 A   7 C   (6 and 7 interchangeable)
8 G   9 H   10 I   (8, 9 and 10 interchangeable)
11 E   12 F   13 H

Second text: 14 D   15 D   16 A   17 C   18 B

Third text: 19 A   20 G   21 E   22 H   23 D   24 F   25 C

Fourth text: 26 H   27 G   28 E   29 D   30 B   31 A
32 A   33 C   34 A   35 B   36 C   37 G   38 E
39 F   40 C

Paper 2 Writing (2 hours)

See pages 9–18 for assessment criteria and sample answers.

Paper 3 English in Use (1 hour 30 minutes)

Section A

Question 1 [One mark for each correct answer]
1 A   2 D   3 B   4 B   5 A   6 B   7 C   8 A   9 C
10 A   11 B   12 B   13 D   14 B   15 A

Question 2 [One mark for each correct answer]
16 for/when   17 One   18 either/whether   19 is   20 the
21 other   22 many   23 who   24 even/in   25 but   26 the
27 back   28 are   29 to   30 those

35

Practice Test 2

Section B

Question 3 [One mark for each correct answer]

31 ✓ 32 case 33 had 34 made 35 seeing 36 ✓
37 more 38 collectors 39 promising 40 Later 41 sent
42 botanist 43 ✓

Question 4 [One mark for each correct answer]

44 welcomed/greeted 45 discussion/conversation 46 was shown
47 student accommodation/rooms 48 was provided/prepared
49 praised 50 compared 51 visited two/some 52 his attention
53 condition/state 54 a need/case 55 (every) reason/cause

Section C

Question 5 [One mark for each correct answer]

56 E 57 G 58 H 59 I 60 B 61 A

Question 6 [These are specimen answers – up to two marks for each sentence]

81 I suggest you do a rice salad, which is easy to make and tasty, but not too expensive.
82 All you need is lots of colourful vegetables, like carrots and peppers, and some onion, cut into small chunks, rice, and salad dressing.
83 Using a large, heavy pan, soften the vegetables in oil or butter for five minutes.
84 Add water, rice and salt and cook it until the rice is done.
85 Meanwhile, make a salad dressing by mixing lemon juice or vinegar with oil (olive if you have it), mustard and pepper.
86 Rinse the rice and vegetables in hot water, and then, before they cool, add the dressing, stirring well.
87 This is also very good if you add things like chopped nuts, eggs or cheese at the same time as the dressing.

Paper 4 Listening (45 minutes)

Section A [One mark for each correct answer]

1 New Zealand 2 farm (house) 3 Festival 4 posters 5 printer
6 Late Flowering 7 Hensham Community Centre 8 3–9 August
9 13.45 / 1.45 / quarter to two

Section B [One mark for each correct answer]

10 waterproof 11 hood 12 frame 13 sweets/chocolate
14 cans (of drink) 15 small notebooks 16 envelope

Practice Test 2

Section C [One mark for each correct answer]

17 R   18 N   19 O   20 R   21 O   22 O   23 R   24 N
25 R   26 O

Section D [One mark for each correct answer]

27 B   28 C   29 A   30 F   31 H   32 A   33 C   34 D
35 F   36 G

Transcript

This is the Certificate in Advanced English, Listening Test. Practice Test number 2. There are four sections to the test, A, B, C and D. You will hear Section B once only. All the other parts of the test will be heard twice. During the test, there will be a pause before each part to allow you to look through the questions, and other pauses to let you think about your answers. At the end of every pause you will hear this sound.

tone

You should write your answers on the question paper. You will have ten minutes at the end to transfer your answers to the separate answer sheet. The tape will now be stopped. You must ask any questions now, as you will not be allowed to speak during the test.

[*pause*]

Section A. Candy Watkins works in the tourist office of a small town in the West of England. Each morning her first job is to check the messages on the telephone answering machine for her boss, Heather. Look at her notes below and complete the information for questions 1–9. You will hear the recording twice.

[*pause*]

tone

V1: [answerphone] This is Hensham Tourist Office. We are sorry there is no one to take your call at the moment. Please leave a message after the tone, or call again during office opening hours, which are 9.30 to 4, Monday to Friday. Thank you.

V2: Oh, eh, this is er, Ed Benkel here. Erm, we'd like, er that is, the wife and I, er, that's, Mr and Mrs Benkel, er, we'd like to make a booking through you, er, we're over from New Zealand and we want to stay in Hensham for three nights, er, in bed and breakfast, er, we'd like to stay in a farmhouse, er, not in the town, er, starting Friday. Can you fix that? Er, I'll call you tomorrow to confirm. Thank you.

V3: Durham here. Monty Durham. Henmouth Festival Office. Right. We've got the posters for the festival. That is, the printer fellow's got 'em. He'll deliver direct to you, save a lot of hassle. So, question is, how many do you want? Okey-dokey? Be in touch.

V4: Erm, I'm phoning on behalf of Oxbow Players, er, you know, drama group? You very kindly agreed, erm, to publicise our production this summer, so I'm phoning to tell you, erm, about it. Erm, it's called 'Late Flowering', it's a

Practice Test 2

comedy, at least it's supposed to be. We'll be doing it at the usual venue, that's Hensham Community Centre of course, and er, thank you for er – oh, yes, it'll be the third to the ninth of August. Er, thank you very much.

V5: Erm, Mum? I mean, Candy, can you let Mum, I mean Heather, know that I'll be late? They've changed the time of my driving lesson from half past ten to half past twelve, so I'll get the eleven o'clock bus, but I want a lift home so I'll come to the office at quarter to two, so can you, I mean she, wait for me? Thanks.

[*pause*]

tone

Now you will hear the piece again. [The recording is repeated.]

[*pause*]

That is the end of Section A.

[*pause*]

Section B. You will hear a college tutor giving some information to a group of students about arrangements for a field trip. As you listen, fill in the information on the booking forms for questions 10–16. Listen very carefully as you will hear this piece only once.

[*pause*]

tone

Tutor: Thank you all for coming in. I just want to run through a few details about the field trip at the beginning of next term. It's mainly things you need, I thought perhaps you could get them together over the vacation. Anyway, erm, first of all, yes, clothing. Obviously we'll be in some pretty damp spots, so the most important thing, and this really is a must, is waterproof gear for your feet. It doesn't really matter whether that's gumboots, or climbing boots, or whatever, as long as they don't let the wet in. It's also going to rain some of the time, so can I urge you to find yourself a jacket that has an integral hood? There's nothing more miserable than trying to do research with cold water running down the back of your neck, and really a hood's the only thing. And it can't get lost like a hat can.

Now, bags. I realise you won't all have one, but if you can borrow, or even hire, a backpack which has a frame, you'll save yourself a lot of backache. The frame makes all the difference when you're carrying it some distance.

Then, what else? Oh, yes. A do and a don't. Do fix yourself up with a few packets of sweets. There's nowhere to buy them, and a bar of chocolate or something is a real treat when you're cold and wet and two miles from base. On the other hand, don't bring canned drinks. There is a supply provided, anyway, and cans are much too heavy to carry all that way.

Lastly, just an idea about stationery. The best thing is to bring a couple of fairly small notebooks rather than the sort of big files we usually use. Something that'll go in your pocket. And also, and I expect you've already got something that'll do, bring a clear plastic envelope or something like that to keep the notebooks in. Otherwise you risk losing all your notes to the rain! OK. Any questions about any of that, or the travel arrangements ...

[*pause*]

That is the end of Section B.

[*pause*]

Section C. You will hear a discussion between three people, Ray, Nonna and Owen, who are talking about the problems they have in travelling around the city where they live. For questions 17–26, indicate which solutions are proposed by each speaker. Write R for Ray, N for Nonna, or O for Owen in the box provided. You should write one initial only for each answer. You will hear the piece twice.

[*pause*]

tone

Nonna: Hi, Ray.
Owen: Hallo Ray, something wrong?
Ray: Hi Nonna. Hell, this traffic. If they don't do something soon I'm going to find a job somewhere else!
Owen: Here, have a coffee.
Nonna: What is it today? The roundabout?
Ray: Thanks, Owen. Yeah, they've got to separate out the bikes on main roads. It's suicide in the rush hour. It wouldn't be difficult to make lanes at the side where cyclists'd be safe. On big roads, anyway.
Nonna: But there'd still be the juggernauts thundering alongside if they did that. Wouldn't it make more sense to have routes right away from the motor traffic?
Owen: Yes, but who's going to be prepared to cycle farther?
Nonna: Well, me, Owen, for one, if I felt safer.
Owen: But Nonna, you never go past the end of this road. It's energy you want, not safety. What people like you would really benefit from would be one of those schemes where you can park your bike or car on the outskirts and then get a cheap bus into the centre.
Nonna: Yeah, park and ride, aren't they usually called?
Owen: I think that's it, yeah.
Ray: I don't think people'd use it unless it was really cheap. Now if they were free ...
Nonna: Oh, yeah, Ray very likely!
Ray: But if you didn't have to pay fares, everyone'd use the buses, then there'd be no congestion, bikes'd be safe ...
Owen: Yes, but who'd pay for the buses?
Nonna: And who'd bother to bike if the bus was free?
Ray: People who needed to lose weight!
Nonna: Watch it, you!
Owen: But seriously, it would help if bus fares weren't so high. It would encourage more people to use them, don't you think?
Ray: Well, anything would help. You mean special fares for pensioners and so on?
Owen: Well, I was thinking if government put some money up, like they do in some countries, so the fares could be kept low.
Ray: I can see this lot doing that.
Owen: And another thing is we need a lot more car parks ...

Practice Test 2

Nonna: But where can we put them? Half the centre's a conservation area, they can't knock it down for car parks.
Owen: But there's no reason why they shouldn't go under the centre.
Ray: Plenty of other places have underground car parks.
Nonna: Ugh. No. They always seem very sinister to me. And they'd cost a fortune to build.
Ray: Well, if it costs a lot to park, people wouldn't bring cars into the centre, so that'd help too. I think that's a good idea. If you can afford a car you can afford to …
Owen: Don't be daft, Ray. Just because you haven't got one yourself. But I agree they would be costly to construct.
Nonna: Well, I think it'd save a lot of hassle if they just kept vehicles out of the centre all together.
Ray: Lovely, yeah, just turn the whole place into a great mall.
Owen: Well, at least people'd still be able to shop there. It'll die if they don't do something soon.
Ray: So what? We could leave it to the banks and the tourists. If the suburban railway was modernised, and subsidised …
Nonna: Yes.
Ray: … and extended so it covered all the city, we could all get about easily …
Nonna: You're talking nonsense …
Owen: But where would you find space for new lines Ray?
Ray: Where roads are now.
Nonna: Ray, do be practical.
Ray: Why not?
Owen: Unless they put them underneath … after all, you don't have to be a capital to have an underground …
Nonna: But, Owen, the cost would be horrendous!
Ray: Yeah, of course.
Nonna: Oh, come on, Ray!
Owen: You're hopeless. Look, let's go down and get a take-away …
Ray: All right. But I'm right, you'll see, it'll take a while …

[*pause*]

tone

Now you will hear the piece again. [The recording is repeated.]

[*pause*]

That is the end of Section C.

[*pause*]

Now look at Section D for the fourth and last part of the test. You will hear extracts of five different people talking. They are all talking about something to do with health. Look at Task One. Letters A–H list various different people. As you listen, put them in order by completing the boxes numbered 27–31 with the appropriate letter. Now look at Task Two. Letters A–H list the purposes of the people speaking in the extracts. As you listen, put them in order by completing the boxes numbered 32–36 with the appropriate letter. You will hear the series twice.

[*pause*]

tone

Student: Look, I'm really very sorry, but, well, I've got this awful headache, and my throat feels all kind of well, tender, when I swallow, I just can't think straight. So anyway I'm afraid the point is, well I haven't been able to do my assignment yet. I'm terribly sorry.

Surgeon: Now what we want to do, given that you're still bothered with this abdominal discomfort, and we haven't found anything in our tests which accounts for it satisfactorily, what we'd like to do, is, just make a small incision which would enable us to have a quick look round. It'd only take a few minutes, but I think it'd save you worrying. Don't you think that might be a good idea?

Parent: I'm sorry to bother you again, the thing is, you know you said I should call if her temperature rose, and it has and she seems to be breathing very fast. She had some of that medicine about an hour ago. Do you think I should give her some more, or had you better see her? I don't want to give you an unnecessary journey, but, well, she's so little, I don't like to take her out in this weather, not with such a high temperature.

Employer: I'm so very sorry to hear about your daughter. It must be very distressing for you. Now what I want you to understand is that when you need time to take her to the clinic for treatment or whatever, you are to take it. OK? I'm going to have a word with your line manager, so she can arrange cover. You don't need to ask permission every time. OK? We all feel for you about this, and we want to help however we can.

Dentist: Well, now I'm afraid it's a bit of a hassle, but I think the best thing for you to do, rather than have me writing letters and so on, which will only slow things up, is for you to contact the hospital yourself. Explain the problem with your jaw, tell them I've seen it and confirmed that it's not the teeth, they're all in reasonable condition, and see what they say. Then if they aren't helpful you can refer them to me and I'll see what I can do.

[*pause*]

tone

Now you will hear the piece again. [The recording is repeated.]

[*pause*]

That is the end of Section D. There will now be a ten-minute pause for you to transfer your answers to the separate answer sheet. Be sure to follow the numbering of all the questions. The question papers and answer sheets will then be collected by your supervisor.

[*pause*]

That is the end of the test.

Practice Test 2

Paper 5 Speaking   (15 minutes)

Note: In the examination, there will be both an assessor and an interlocutor in the room. The following notes use plural forms where appropriate, although we realise a teacher may often be working alone for practice sessions.
You will need to refer to Paper 5 of Practice Test 2 in the Student's Book and the colour section 'Visual materials for Paper 5' also in the Student's Book.

Phase A   (approximately three minutes)

INTRODUCTIONS

>Good morning. My name is ... and this is my colleague ...
>And your names are?
>First of all we'd like to know a little about you. Do you know each other?

If yes:
>In that case, perhaps you (*Candidate A*) would like to tell us a little about (*Candidate B*) – where (s)he's from, what his/her hobbies and interests are, what (s)he does, *etc.*
>And (*Candidate B*), would you like to introduce us to (*Candidate A*) now, please?
>How long have you known each other?
>(*If applicable:*)
>What do you know about each other's country?

If no:
>Could you please find out about each other? Ask each other where you're from, what you're interested in, how you like to spend your time, why you're learning English, your plans for the future, your families, what you do, *etc.* (*select as applicable*)

GENERAL SOCIAL CONVERSATION

If in UK:
>(*Candidate A*), could you tell (*Candidate B*) what it's like to live in ...
>(*Candidate B*), do you think you would like to visit ...?
>(*Candidate B*), could you now tell (*Candidate A*) about where you live?
>How long are you staying here?
>Both of you come from places that are rather different from England. What do you think are the biggest differences?
>Is there anything in particular that you like or dislike about England? *etc.*

In candidates' country:
>Well, you both live here in ... What would you say are the good things about living in ...? Are there any disadvantages?
>How do you get to school/work?
>What is the best way of travelling round here? *etc.*

Phase B (three or four minutes)

1 | CHILD (Spot the difference) |

In this part of the test I'm going to give each of you a picture to look at. Please do not show your pictures to each other.
Indicate child picture 2A to Candidate A and child picture 2B to Candidate B.
Your pictures are very similar but not the same. I'd like you, (*Candidate A*), to describe your picture in detail to (*Candidate B*). Talk about the person and her surroundings. You have about a minute to do this.
I'd like you, (*Candidate B*), to listen very carefully and then tell us three things which are different in your picture. If you are still uncertain when (*Candidate A*) has finished, you may ask him/her a few questions to help you.
All right? So, (*Candidate A*), would you start please?
(*Candidate A speaks for approximately one minute.*)
Thank you. Now, (*Candidate B*), I'd like you to tell us briefly about the differences you identified.
(*Candidate B speaks for approximately 20 seconds.*)
If Candidate B has not identified sufficient differences, ask him/her about some of the similarities.
Thank you very much.
Note: You may wish to allow students to show each other their pictures but under examination conditions, candidates would not be invited to compare pictures at the end of this exercise, for security reasons.

2 | THE OFFICE (Describe and locate) |

Now I'm going to give (*Candidate B*) a picture of an office, and (*Candidate A*) some spare paper and a pencil. (*Candidate B*), please do not show your picture to (*Candidate A*).
Indicate office picture 2C to Candidate B and pass some spare paper and a pencil to Candidate A.
I'd like you, (*Candidate B*), to describe the position of the furniture in this office as clearly as possible so that (*Candidate A*) can draw a plan of where the furniture should be. You have about one minute to do this. (*Candidate A*), please don't worry if you can't draw, you can use symbols or write words if you prefer. All you have to do is indicate where the various pieces of furniture should be in the office. You may like to copy this plan of the room. *Indicate plan of office 2D to Candidate A.*
Do you understand? So, would you like to begin please (*Candidate B*)?
(*Candidate B speaks for approximately one minute.*)
Thank you. Now, (*Candidate A*), could you show (*Candidate B*) your plan and explain briefly where you've put the furniture?
(*Candidate A speaks for approximately 20 seconds.*)
Thank you very much. Now, would you like to compare your pictures?

Practice Test 2

Phase C (three or four minutes)

GADGETS (Evaluate and discuss)

Indicate the set of gadget pictures 2E to the pair of candidates.
I'd like you both to look at these pictures of gadgets. Talk about them, and decide what they're used for, and who might use them. Talk about how practical they are and whether you'd consider buying them, for yourselves or to give to someone else.
You have three or four minutes for this.

Phase D (three or four minutes)

What did you decide about these gadgets?
Are they things people really need?
Do people buy a lot of things they don't need? Why?
What effect can this have on everyday life?
Do you think this is important in global terms? Why?

Practice Test 3

Paper 1 Reading   (1 hour + 15 minutes)

First text: 1 A   2 J   3 C   4 F   5 I   6 E   7 D   8 F
9 B   10 G   11 C   12 I   13 D   14 H

Teachers and students may be interested to know the books referred to in this text.

- A: *Upland Britain* by Margaret Atherden (pub. Manchester University Press)
- B: *Silent Spring* by Rachel Carson (pub. Houghton Mifflin 1962, Penguin 1991)
- C: *Walks to Yorkshire Waterfalls* by Mary Welsh (pub. Cicerone Press)
- D: *Cousteau's Great White Shark* by Jean-Michel Cousteau and Mose Richards (pub. Abrams)
- E: *The Dammed* by Fred Pearce (pub. Jonathan Cape)
- F: *Gaia: A new look at life on Earth* by James Lovelock (pub. Oxford University Press 1979)
- G: *Whale Nation* by Heathcote Williams (pub. Random House UK)
- H: *Standing on Earth* by Wendell Berry (pub. Golgonooza Press 1991)
- I: *The Diversity of Life* by Edward O Wilson (pub. Allen Lane, The Penguin Press)
- J: *The Amateur Naturalist* by Gerald and Lee Durrell (pub. Dorling Kindersley)

Second text: 15 B   16 B   17 A   18 A   19 B

Third text: 20 C   21 F   22 D   23 G   24 E   25 A

Fourth text: 26 B   27 C   28 D   29 F   30 H   (all interchangeable)
31 B   32 C   33 F   (all interchangeable)

Paper 2 Writing   (2 hours)

See pages 9–18 for assessment criteria and sample answers.

Practice Test 3

Paper 3 English in Use (1 hour 30 minutes)

Section A

Question 1   [One mark for each correct answer]

1 D   2 B   3 A   4 A   5 D   6 B   7 A   8 C   9 D
10 C   11 A   12 D   13 B   14 C   15 D

Question 2   [One mark for each correct answer]

16 With   17 most   18 own   19 which   20 an   21 with
22 ever   23 for   24 who   25 of   26 Whether   27 out
28 is   29 may/could   30 by

Section B

Question 3   [One mark for each correct answer]

31 ✓   32 rubbish. The   33 ✓   34 clever," said   35 it's   36 ✓
37 we think we   38 ✓   39 physics   40 technologies, suggest
41 orbiting   42 tortoises. Only   43 may be

Question 4 [One mark for each correct answer]

44 be in   45 received/was given   46 longer   47 not renew/pay
48 continued   49 demand payment   50 ignored
51 a discount/reduction   52 legal   53 being treated   54 assurance

Section C

Question 5   [One mark for each correct answer]

55 A   56 K   57 B   58 J   59 C   60 D   61 G   62 F
63 E

Question 6 [These are specimen answers – up to two marks for each sentence]

81 It is the responsibility of your sponsors to organise and pay for travel to London.
82 Delegates will stay at the Atlantic Hotel, which is five minutes from Lancaster Gate underground station.
83 The cost of travel on the underground is refundable, but taxi fares are not.
84 Please check into the hotel between seven and nine p.m., identifying yourself as a language conference delegate in order to collect your meal vouchers.
85 The main conference centre is Merton Hall, which is situated on the corner of Merton Place.
86 If you are not familiar with London, please ask for directions from the hotel porter.

87 You should arrive at the Hall by 8.30 to allow time for administrative procedures, as the first session will start promptly at 9 a.m.

Paper 4 Listening   (45 minutes)

Section A   [One mark for each correct answer]

1 passage   2 shoulder   3 word processor(s)   4 meeting room/area
5 photocopier   6 ceiling   7 wall/rack   8 external wall

Section B   [One mark for each correct answer]

9 yes   10 no   11 yes   12 no   13 no   14 yes   15 yes
16 yes   17 no

Section C   [One mark for each correct answer]

18 fury/outrage(d)/angry/furious   19 fair/just
20 optimism/see best in everything   21 bravery/courage/willing to take risks
22 let down/disappointed   23 guilty   24 cross/irritated
25 hurt/annoyed/resentful   26 his first wife's mother / his mother-in-law

Section D   [One mark for each correct answer]

27 B   28 F   29 A   30 H   31 C   32 A   33 F   34 C
35 H   36 B

Transcript

This is the Certificate in Advanced English, Listening Test. Practice Test number 3. There are four sections to the test, A, B, C and D. You will hear Section B once only. All the other parts of the test will be heard twice. During the test, there will be a pause before each part to allow you to look through the questions, and other pauses to let you think about your answers. At the end of every pause you will hear this sound.

tone

You should write your answers on the question paper. You will have ten minutes at the end to transfer your answers to the separate answer sheet. The tape will now be stopped. You must ask any questions now, as you will not be allowed to speak during the test.

[pause]

Section A. Jim has called his business partner, Ed, to tell him about some ideas for altering their office. For questions 1–8, listen to what Jim says and complete Ed's notes. You will hear the recording twice.

Practice Test 3

[*pause*]

tone

Jim: Hi. Ed?
Ed: Jim. How're things?
Jim: I've been talking to that office design guy I told you about. He's made a lot of suggestions. I thought I'd relay them to you then you can make a few notes and mull them over, all right?
Ed: Sure.
Jim: Well, first of all, I think he's come up with a way to solve the space problem. He says, what we want to do, is knock down the inner wall of the passage, so we've got one big space. I said we'd thought of that but we didn't want clients bursting straight in on us, and he said, and I think this might work, that if the outer bit, like where they come in, if that was the meeting space, and the far end was our bit, so to speak, we could have a screen to keep us private. Sort of about shoulder height. Then we'd be able to pop our heads up and look, but our work space wouldn't be visible.
Ed: It might work.
Jim: Yeah. Yeah. Then he said if we had one big, like, work surface against the left wall, we could put the word processors on it as well as use it as ordinary desk space.
Ed: What about storage, though?
Jim: Well, we don't need the whole width of the room for the meeting area. We measured it, and he's right, we can easily fit a table and chairs in just over half. So we can have one whole wall in that part covered in deep cupboards.
Ed: Mm.
Jim: Yeah, and then there'll be a nice airy feeling where we work. And we can use the other wall, where the work surface isn't, for the telephone and stuff, and there'd be space for the photocopier along there too, which'd be really handy.
Ed: Won't it all be a bit dark and stuffy?
Jim: That's another thing we talked about. He said what we should do is rewire so we can have a light in the ceiling, and that could be centred over the table for meetings, right? But in the other half, like just above the, you know, work surface, we should have a rack of spotlights set in the wall so they shine on to it. And, and, to keep the place fresh we could have an extractor fan in the external wall. Well, don't you think he's got some good ideas? I told you he knew about these things.
Ed: Mm. Look, I've made some notes. I'll call you tomorrow when I've thought about them, OK?
Jim: OK, then. I'll wait till I hear, shall I?

[*pause*]

tone

Now you will hear the piece again. [The recording is repeated.]

[*pause*]

That is the end of Section A.

[*pause*]

Section B. You will hear a local radio announcement about travel conditions. For questions 9–17 look at the pictures and mark 'yes' the problems which are described. Mark the ones which are not described with 'no'. Listen very carefully as you will hear this piece only once.

[*pause*]

tone

Local radio announcer: … and after the weather we have some information about travel conditions in the area today. Did you hear me say there wasn't much going on, earlier this morning? I take it all back. First of all, for those of you on foot, be prepared to go the long way round at the junction of Gale Street and the ringroad dual carriageway. Vandals have damaged the fencing of the elevated pedestrian walkway there and it has been declared unsafe, so you have to go right round the block at ground level and use the pedestrian crossing. Next, we have news that the airport is still having difficulties as a result of the torrential rain in the storm last week. Power has been restored by means of temporary cables, but pumping work is behind schedule so there is still an area of runway flooded. Services should be resumed tomorrow, but travellers should check by phone before leaving home. Another aftermath of the storm is that the bus stop in Bridge Street is still temporarily at the corner of John Street, as the fallen tree across the pavement has not yet been removed. New work is due to begin later today on the ring road approach to Park Street roundabout, and the road has already been closed. Diversion signs have been posted, but I should think you'd do well to avoid the park area entirely if you can, especially during this evening's rush hour. Lastly, if you're planning to use the car park at the corner of Station Road and Green Street – forget it. Apparently a lorry carrying scrap metal has shed its load right by the car park entrance and it's blocking it completely! What a mess! Well, after that, what we need is some music, and I've got just the thing for all you travellers with frayed nerves …

[*pause*]

That is the end of Section B.

[*pause*]

Section C. You will hear part of a radio programme in which James Clebourne, an award-winning photographer, talks to the presenter, Miranda Day, about his early life and the beginnings of his successful career. For questions 18–26, complete the information according to what James says. You will hear the piece twice.

[*pause*]

tone

Practice Test 3

MD: Hallo. This is Miranda Day, and with me on 'Talk Today' this time is James Clebourne. We've all enjoyed your photographs over the past twenty years or more, James. Did you come from an artistic family?

JC: Thank you, Miranda. Er, well, no I must say I didn't. Erm, I don't really remember my parents, who died in an air crash when I was three, but I think I can safely say that they weren't what is generally meant by 'artistic'.

MD: What sort of people were they?

JC: Well, as I said, I don't actually have any direct memories of them. Erm, they were well off. My father had what in those days was a very highly paid job, and my mother had money of her own. My infancy was charmed I think, er, you know, nanny and nurse maid and, er, the atmosphere of things being ordered for my benefit. It think it must have been that which caused the fury I felt at their deaths. Because I do recall that, although I don't remember them. I was just outraged. How could events have the temerity to turn on me and upset my world? That's how it was.

MD: And did the world change for you materially at that point?

JC: Yes, in fact it did. I had the silver spoon whipped smartly out of my mouth. Erm, my father's family wasn't rich, and his salary died with him. People didn't bother so much with life insurance in those days. Suddenly there was just my mother's pin money. I went to live with my father's brother and his wife. They were good people, schoolteachers, but quite different from my parents.

MD: In their attitudes as well as their style of life?

JC: Absolutely. They lacked the energy, the excitement of my parents and their friends. Rather puritanical, duty before pleasure, quite severe in their attitudes to human weaknesses. They made a good job of my upbringing though – erm, of course I suppose that's hardly for me to say, but you know what I mean – erm, I had to do as I was told. But they were scrupulously fair. One rarely had a sense of injustice about punishments for example.

MD: So do you think you inherited your personality from your parents, or can't you tell?

JC: Well, my father was always one to see the best side of everything, that's what everyone always told me who knew him. And that made him very positive in his work. I think I'm an optimist, that's one of the things that's helped me get on in my work. I guess we must have been quite alike in that.

MD: And your mother? Were your parents similar, do you know?

JC: Fairly, I should imagine. What I've always thought about her, is that she must've been quite brave, someone who would take risks. I suspect her family thought she took one when she married my father, and I guess I've taken a few over the years.

MD: In your career, you mean, for example?

JC: Yes. I don't say I'm a lot braver than plenty of other people. But one takes quite a bit of flak in a career like photography, especially if it's not the sort of thing one's family has gone in for.

MD: Did your family, your aunt and uncle, disapprove of your career choice?

JC: Erm, I suppose you could say that. I think my uncle, er, well, both of them, had hoped I would go to university and so on. But my uncle, he just sort of talked in a way, nothing direct, but he felt, er, obviously, I guess, a bit let down because, er, it wasn't what he'd hoped. Erm, but he didn't criticise me to my face.

MD: But your aunt?

JC: She said more. She minded that I hadn't taken their advice, and, er, made it abundantly clear in fact. And that lasted a long time.

MD: And you minded that?

50

JC: At first I did. I suffered terrible pangs of conscience that I had upset these people who'd been so good to me. Er, because they had, in their own way. As time went on and I began to make my mark in the field I'd chosen, I stopped feeling so guilty. Erm, I soon got back on terms with my uncle and just felt cross that they'd been holding something so unreasonable against me. It irritated me that they, at first, and latterly my aunt, should go on being so resentful after I'd been proved right. Erm, but that's a long way past, now, of course.

MD: You're still close?

JC: When I got married to my first wife, er, well that was a mistake, was one very good outcome in that I made a friend, my wife's mother, in fact, who is still a friend to me today. And before we got married, she took it into her head to sort out the bad feeling, er, said it would blight the marriage, etc. Erm, of course it was blighted anyway, we all found that out soon enough, but anyway, apart from her friendship, getting me and my aunt back so we trusted each other again, that was the best thing that happened around that marriage.

MD: And did it leave you scarred, the experience of a broken marriage, do you think, or …

[*pause*]

tone

Now you will hear the piece again. [The recording is repeated.]

[*pause*]

That is the end of Section C.

[*pause*]

Now look at Section D for the fourth and last part of the test. You will hear extracts of five different people talking about a near disaster at an airport. A plane which was approaching the area had to make an emergency landing in poor weather conditions. The people are describing how the event affected them. Look at Task One. Letters A–H list various different people. As you listen, put them in order by completing the boxes numbered 27–31 with the appropriate letter. Now look at Task Two. Letters A–H list the main ideas expressed by the speakers. As you listen, put them in order by completing the boxes numbered 32–36 with the appropriate letter. You will hear the series twice.

[*pause*]

tone

Passenger: It was incredible, everything happened so fast, one minute we were in the air, the next we'd landed. To be honest I thought they'd just forgotten to do some of the routine things. None of us had any idea we'd been in danger till we were out on the ground. The crew were wonderful, they all knew just what to do, they kept calm and just made it all seem like part of the normal routine.

Restaurant manager: Well, what can we do? I can't have half a dozen extra waiters standing around every day on the off chance we'll have have a sudden rush, can I? These franchises are very tightly financed,

Practice Test 3

	we have to keep our costs right down or we can't operate. People complain enough already at the prices we have to charge, and if that means queues when there's been some sort of hold-up, there's not much we can do about it. I mean, contingency plans would mean staff on standby and as I say, we're not making the sort of profits that'd let us do that, are we now?
Pilot:	Erm, I found, er, we had this problem, er, with one of the engines, so er, I contacted flight control again a bit sharpish, and er, they set it up, so I could go into the standard routine for such a situation, and erm, down we came. All very smooth luckily.
Customs officer:	It was just chaos in here. They'd had so many flights on hold we just had this great stream coming through. We'd been standing around for hours, and half the shift had gone home, so there was no way we could do the usual number of searches. God only knows what they got through. It must have been a dream come true for the smugglers.
Steward:	You know you go through it all so many times in your training, when you get to the real thing, it takes a while to cotton on that this is for real and there's actual danger and by then you're so busy it's just get through the work, get the passengers ready for emergency landing, make sure they're not panicking, keep looking calm, and before you know it, you're on the tarmac with shaking legs and you think, Wow! that would have been frightening if I'd had a chance to think about it.

[*pause*]

tone

Now you will hear the piece again. [The recording is repeated.]

[*pause*]

That is the end of Section D. There will now be a ten-minute pause for you to transfer your answers to the separate answer sheet. Be sure to follow the numbering of all the questions. The question papers and answer sheets will then be collected by your supervisor.

[*pause*]

That is the end of the test.

Paper 5 Speaking   (15 minutes)

Note: In the examination, there will be both an assessor and an interlocutor in the room. The following notes use plural forms where appropriate, although we realise a teacher may often be working alone for practice sessions.
You will need to refer to Paper 5 of Practice Test 3 in the Student's Book and the colour section 'Visual materials for Paper 5' also in the Student's Book.

Phase A   (approximately three minutes)

INTRODUCTIONS

Good morning. My name is ... and this is my colleague ...
And your names are?
First of all we'd like to know a little about you. Do you know each other?

If yes:
In that case, perhaps you (*Candidate A*) would like to tell us a little about (*Candidate B*) – where (s)he's from, what his/her hobbies and interests are, what (s)he does, *etc*.
And (*Candidate B*), would you like to introduce us to (*Candidate A*) now, please?
How long have you known each other?
(*If applicable:*)
What do you know about each other's country?

If no:
Could you please find out about each other? Ask each other where you're from, what you're interested in, how you like to spend your time, why you're learning English, your plans for the future, your families, what you do, *etc*. (select as applicable)

GENERAL SOCIAL CONVERSATION

If in UK:
(*Candidate A*), could you tell (*Candidate B*) what it's like to live in ...
(*Candidate B*), do you think you would like to visit ...?
(*Candidate B*), could you now tell (*Candidate A*) about where you live?
How long are you staying here?
Both of you come from places that are rather different from England. What do you think are the biggest differences?
Is there anything in particular that you like or dislike about England? *etc*.

In candidates' country:
Well, you both live here in ... What would you say are the good things about living in ...? Are there any disadvantages?
How do you get to school/work?
What is the best way of travelling round here? *etc*.

Practice Test 3

Phase B   (three or four minutes)

1   FITNESS CENTRE (Spot the difference)

In this part of the test I'm going to give you each a picture to look at. Please do not show your pictures to each other.
Indicate fitness centre picture 3A to Candidate A and fitness centre picture 3B to Candidate B.
Your pictures are very similar but not the same. I'd like you, (*Candidate A*), to describe your picture in detail to (*Candidate B*). Talk about the people and their surroundings. You have about a minute to do this.
I'd like you, (*Candidate B*), to listen very carefully and then tell us three things which are different in your picture. If you are still uncertain when (*Candidate A*) has finished, you may ask him/her a few questions to help you.
All right? So, (*Candidate A*), would you start please?
(*Candidate A speaks for approximately one minute.*)
Thank you. Now (*Candidate B*), I'd like you to tell us briefly about the differences you identified.
(*Candidate B speaks for approximately 20 seconds.*)
If candidate B has not identified sufficient differences, ask him/her about some of the similarities.
Thank you very much.
Note: You may wish to allow students to compare their pictures but under examination conditions, candidates would not be invited to compare pictures at the end of this exercise, for security reasons.

2   YOGA (Describe and identify)

Now I'm going to give each of you some pictures of someone doing yoga. Please do not show your pictures to each other.
Indicate yoga set 3C to Candidate B and yoga set 3D to Candidate A.
(*Candidate B*) has five pictures, but you, (*Candidate A*), have six. I'd like you, (*Candidate B*), to describe as clearly as you can each of these positions. Say whether you think it's comfortable or not, or whether it looks easy to hold. You have about one minute to do this. After that I shall ask you, (*Candidate A*), to describe the remaining position on your page. Here is some spare paper if you need to make any notes. *Hand over pencil and paper.*
Do you understand? So, would you like to begin please (*Candidate B*)?
(*Candidate B speaks for approximately one minute.*)
Thank you. Now, (*Candidate A*), could you describe the extra position on your page, please?
(*Candidate A speaks for approximately 20 seconds.*)
Thank you. Would you like to compare your pages now and check whether you identified the positions correctly?

Phase C   (three or four minutes)

> HOLIDAY PRIZE (Select and discard)

Indicate holiday adverts 3E to the pair of candidates.
You have been asked to choose one of these holidays to award as a prize for a competition for young writers. Talk about which holiday would attract most people to enter the competition and why. If you don't both choose the same one, ask each other to justify your choice. If you do agree, discuss why the others would be less suitable.
You have three or four minutes for this.

Phase D   (three or four minutes)

Which holiday did you choose? Why?
Would you enter such a competition? Why?
What sort of people would you expect to be travelling with if you went on any of these holidays?
These are very different sorts of places, can you say what sort of effect tourists might have on each of them?
Should there be some places which tourists can't visit? Why?

Practice Test 4

Paper 1 Reading (1 hour + 15 minutes)

First text: 1 A   2 C   3 H   (1, 2 and 3 interchangeable)
               4 F   5 G   (4 and 5 interchangeable)
               6 B   7 C   8 E   (6, 7 and 8 interchangeable)
               9 B   10 A   11 C   12 E   13 D
Second text: 14 C   15 A   16 D   17 B   18 C   19 A
Third text: 20 E   21 F   22 A   23 C   24 D
Fourth text: 25 E   26 A   27 D   28 B   29 F   30 B
               31 C   32 D   33 F   (31, 32 and 33 interchangeable)
               34 E   35 A   36 B   37 D   (35, 36 and 37 interchangeable)

Paper 2 Writing (2 hours)

See pages 9–18 for assessment criteria and sample answers.

Paper 3 English in Use (1 hour 30 minutes)

Section A

Question 1 [One mark for each correct answer]

1 B   2 C   3 D   4 A   5 B   6 A   7 C   8 D   9 B
10 C   11 A   12 D   13 A   14 C   15 B

Question 2 [One mark for each correct answer]

16 even/still/much/far   17 to   18 you   19 up   20 whether/if
21 with   22 or   23 same   24 not   25 Some
26 while/but/whereas   27 worth   28 what   29 without
30 which

Section B

Question 3 [One mark for each correct answer]

31 his   32 ✓   33 so   34 if   35 feel   36 for   37 this
38 which   39 ✓   40 something   41 The   42 such

Practice Test 4

Question 4   [One mark for each correct answer]

43 overtime   44 good idea   45 didn't want   46 round/near
47 amount of / bit of   48 coming up   49 even though   50 against
51 no chance / no hope   52 a circle   53 got off   54 even though
55 piece   56 apart from / except for

Section C

Question 5   [One mark for each correct answer]

57 C   58 B   59 D   60 J   61 G   62 H   63 F

Question 6   [These are specimen answers – up to two marks for each sentence]

81 There is evidence that the pottery industry existed in the 14th century.
82 In the 17th century most of the pottery produced was for local use.
83 With the new fashion of tea-drinking came an increased demand for articles such as tea cups.
84 The 18th century saw the development of more refined pottery by Staffordshire potters such as Wedgwood and Spode.
85 Their designs showed the influence of recent excavations in Italy and imports from China.
86 At the same time, canals offered improved communications and Staffordshire pottery was exported.
87 Nowadays, Staffordshire pottery is still popular and commands high prices at auctions of antiques.

Paper 4 Listening   (45 minutes)

Section A   [One mark for each correct answer]

1 North(ern)(of)   2 taking (it) apart/to pieces/bits
3 (working) petrol engine   4 steam   5 garden shed   6 kitchen (sink)
7 test engines/cars   8 engine   9 frozen lake   10 91.37

Section B   [One mark for each correct answer]

11 interpreter   12 Engineering   13 hotel   14 Communications
15 ceramics/pottery   16 Electronics   17 Friendship Store

Section C   [One mark for each correct answer]

18 B   19 D   20 D   21 A   22 B

Section D   [One mark for each correct answer]

23 A   24 B   25 F   26 D   27 E   28 H   29 F   30 E   31 A
32 B

57

Practice Test 4

Transcript

This is the Certificate in Advanced English, Listening Test. Practice Test number 4. There are four sections to the test, A, B, C and D. You will hear Section B once only. All the other parts of the test will be heard twice. During the test, there will be a pause before each part to allow you to look through the questions, and other pauses to let you think about your answers. At the end of every pause you will hear this sound.

tone

You should write your answers on the question paper. You will have ten minutes at the end to transfer your answers to the separate answer sheet. The tape will now be stopped. You must ask any questions now, as you will not be allowed to speak during the test.

[pause]

Section A. For questions 1–10 you will hear a student telling her class about Henry Ford, the inventor. As you listen, complete the information in the notes. You will hear the recording twice.

[pause]

tone

Student: As part of my project on the development of the er, internal combustion engine, erm, I've been finding out about Henry Ford, who bears much of the resonsibility for the early years. Well, he was born in 1863, in the northern United States. He was obviously of a mechanical turn of mind, he enjoyed messing around with farm machinery, taking it to bits and seeing how it worked and so on, even when he was just a kid. Anyway, he grew up, got married when he was in his early twenties, and erm, then he saw a working petrol engine and this really set him off. Because up till then, really, horseless carriages, well, that's what they were known as, were generally powered by steam, or sometimes electricity. What Ford did, was to harness the petrol engine to power a vehicle. He got a job with the Edison Electrical Company and at nights he worked, I think he was pretty obsessed really, so he er, worked in his garden shed. And, er, by the end of 1883, he'd managed to get his first rudimentary engine to fire and run, with his wife dripping in the fuel and him pushing the starting wheel, while it stood propped in the kitchen sink. And after that, there was no stopping him. By 1896, he'd got something he could drive about, which he called the er, Quadricycle, because it was basically a four-wheel bicycle, if you see what I mean, with an engine. In 1898 he started racing cars, he was going on building new ones, trying to improve them and he got into the racing so he could use it to test out what they could do. Well because he couldn't really push them to, you know, the limits on ordinary roads. The first one ever held in Detroit, he won, but it was really dangerous. His average speed was, er, forty-four point eight miles per hour, and he was doing that sitting on a seat right on top of the engine, and with no brakes. I think he must've been a bit mad. Anyway he went on, and, er, in 1904 he got the world speed record, and er, he was driving between banks of snow on a frozen lake, er on a track made of ashes to stop skidding, except it didn't all the time, but anyway, he did ninety-one point three seven miles per hour. I think that was pretty incredible. Anyway, meanwhile, the motor business was beginning to get organised ...

[*pause*]

tone

Now you will hear the piece again. [The recording is repeated.]

[*pause*]

That is the end of Section A.

[*pause*]

Section B. You will hear a man confirming details of a business trip to China for his boss. For questions 11–17, complete the schedule for the trip. Listen very carefully as you will hear this piece only once.

[*pause*]

tone

Man: Hi, Janie, have you got the details for Margaret's China trip yet? [*pause*] Great, I'll get them down then. Now, she's flying to Hong Kong, then transferring, I've got the flights in the agency memo. And she's being met at Shanghai by a Mr Liu, right? Do we know who he is? [*pause*] Oh the interpreter? Well, that should be OK, at least he'll be able to talk English. That makes things easier. And he'll take her to wherever it is she's staying? [*pause*] Great. The Peace Hotel, like opposite of war? Fine. That'll be in the evening. What happens Wednesday then? She's got to go to a meeting at the university, hasn't she? Do we know where? [*pause*] I mean the university's probably got a lot of different departments, hasn't it? [*pause*] Oh, Engineering? Right, and how will she find it? [*pause*] I mean, has she got to be able to direct a taxi driver? [*pause*] So the hotel will see he knows where to go? Oh, fine. And then there's this lunch with some Committee? Communications Committee? [*pause*] Yes, that's what I thought. And then this Mr Liu is taking her to a Museum. Any idea what she'll see? [*pause*] Oh yes, she's very keen on pottery and paintings and things. That's nice of them. I imagine Chinese ceramics will be right up her street. And she's free in the evening, I expect she'll be glad to relax. She's got a long day on Thursday at this industrial place. Do we have a name for it? [*pause*] Well, if we don't know the Chinese, we'll put Electronics [*pause*] oh, that's what it is? This'll be the main meeting then. Will Mr Liu take her there, do you think? [*pause*] Uhuh. Eight o'clock from her hotel. Fine. And then Friday she leaves. What time'll she have to leave the hotel? [*pause*] Uhuh. So she can nip out and do a bit of shopping at the Friendship Store as long as she's ready to go by eleven? [*pause*] Uhuh. I'll tell her the Friendship Store's just by the hotel. Great. I'm sure she'll be relieved to hear it's all so well-planned. [*pause*] Thanks. See you.

[*pause*]

That is the end of Section B.

Practice Test 4

[*pause*]

Section C. You will hear an excerpt from a radio programme, 'Business Matters', in which Shirley, a woman whose business partner disappeared with all their money, discusses her experiences. For questions 18–22 you must choose the best answer A, B, C or D. You will hear the piece twice.

[*pause*]

tone

Presenter: ... and now on 'Business Matters' we come to this week's case study. And this week we talk to Shirley Kildare, who has been through one of those nightmare experiences that we all think could only happen to others. Isn't that right, Shirley?

Shirley: Absolutely. It'd been such fun setting things up, and everything had been going really well, I mean, we started making a profit almost immediately, supplying these handmade chocolates to hotels and delis and so on, you know. I was quite surprised, I thought it'd take years to get known and so on, but we just caught a fashion. Anyway, when Nick did a bunk ...

Presenter: He just disappeared?

Shirley: Just like that. I was devastated. How could he do it, I thought, after all our hard work together? I mean, we'd both worked hard, that was why I felt he was such a traitor, he'd let himself down, and he'd let me down.

Presenter: In different ways.

Shirley: Oh yes. To himself I suppose it was, well, it was a moral betrayal, but me, well, it was theft of course, literally, apart from everything else.

Presenter: What did he take?

Shirley: Everything. Absolutely every penny we had in the business. The bank account was empty. So I went straight round to the lawyers, and said, 'What can I do to get it back?' I had no idea ...

Presenter: Was there nothing to be done?

Shirley: Well, no. Apparently not. We looked at the bits of paper, contracts and things, the lawyer was as horrified as I was. I still can't really take it in. But there you are. There was something we hadn't foreseen when we'd set the business up.

Presenter: So what did you do?

Shirley: What could I do? I sent the girls home from the workshop. I used what savings I had to help one or two of them who were most hard hit. Closed it up. Tried to sell the lease on the premises. My husband was in the States on a long contract. He offered to come back, but what could he have done? I was pretty depressed actually. My daughter wanted me to go to the doctor about it. I got through it though. One has to, in the end. There's an old lady who lives just up the road, she's all on her own, and I used to go and talk to her, just to give her company, and then one day I realised it was actually almost like a sort of therapy for me. You know, she was someone to lean on, to pour it all out to. I've got used to the idea, it's a closed chapter. I'm lucky not to have lost anything more than money. And a bit of self-esteem, I suppose.

Presenter: What about your partner? Have you given up hope of catching up with him?

60

Shirley: To be honest, I'm not sure I want to. I'd like my money back of course, but to have to face him again …
Presenter: Is it not a police matter?
Shirley: Oh, they did make quite strenuous efforts. We know where he left the country from, and they discovered a lot about him that we hadn't known, a few pretty unsavoury haunts, places he'd lived, businesses he'd been involved in, dicey accommodation addresses, that sort of thing. Where he's got to now, I haven't the foggiest. He might be back here living up the road for all I know!
Presenter: So what's next? Have you started anything new?
Shirley: Well – I've had a lot of good advice, a bit late most of it. I don't think I'll take on another partner, unless it was my husband or something! Actually, I'm still feeling pretty shattered, it's like convalescing from an illness really. I don't think I'm ready to call a halt completely, though. I, erm, well, I could retrain, get myself some more skills. But most probably I'll try and find myself a niche in someone else's company. And that'll help me relax a bit!
Presenter: Well, good luck Shirley, whatever you do. And thank you for sharing your experiences with us. Now let's turn to Bill Walters, our legal expert, and see what he has to say about ways of avoiding the problems that Shirley's encountered.

[*pause*]

tone

Now you will hear the piece again. [The recording is repeated.]

[*pause*]

That is the end of Section C.

[*pause*]

Now look at Section D for the fourth and last part of the test. You will hear extracts of five different people talking. They are all talking about some means of transport. Look at Task One. Pictures A–H show various different forms of transport. As you listen, put them in order by completing the boxes numbered 23–27 with the appropriate letter. Now look at Task Two. Letters A–H list the different feelings described by the people speaking in the extracts. As you listen, put them in order by completing the boxes numbered 28–32 with the appropriate letter. You will hear the series twice.

[*pause*]

tone

Elderly man: It was like travelling with a maniac. He'd never used manual gears before, and he thought the speedometer showed kilometres, so we were going at these breakneck speeds. I was beside myself with terror. I almost wished a police car would appear! I've never been so grateful to get to the end of a journey.

Young woman: How they're allowed to get away with it beats me. I mean, they charge enough. It's always too late or too early, the drivers don't know the routes. And you see in the paper all these profits they make, but they can't afford to get a new design that makes it easier

Practice Test 4

	to get on and off. I think it's disgusting. You can tell the bosses don't go to work on them – they'd never put up with it like we have to.
Child:	It was amazing. We started at this place, Angleside, which had everything just like it really was, with the porters and ticket men in old-fashioned uniforms, and there was a buffet with tea and cakes, no burger bars or anything. And they had funny little cardboard sort of tickets. And the engine was beautiful, and it all smelt really old-fashioned. And then we had this compartment all to ourselves, with luggage racks made of sort of netting. It was like something on telly. And when we went through the tunnel, they blew the whistle, and all this sooty stuff came in the windows.
Man:	I was doing fine till I discovered I'd left my wallet at the guesthouse. Well, there was nothing for it but to pedal all the way back. And nearly all uphill. I guess my legs were prepared for fifteen kilometres or so, but the trouble was we were more than halfway before I realised so it was more like twenty-five in the end. I was so shattered I could hardly totter through the door when we finally got home.
Woman:	It's just like part of a different world. Well, I guess that's what it is, isn't it? You just lay back and feel the breeze on your face. And you hear the birds, and the hooves on the track, and the rattle of the harness just every so often, as the driver flicks the reins. You wouldn't want to do it in bad weather, but it's the most peaceful thing going when it's fine.

[*pause*]

tone

Now you will hear the piece again. [The recording is repeated.]

[*pause*]

That is the end of Section D. There will now be a ten-minute pause for you to transfer your answers to the separate answer sheet. Be sure to follow the numbering of all the questions. The question papers and answer sheets will then be collected by your supervisor.

[*pause*]

That is the end of the test.

Paper 5 Speaking (15 minutes)

Note: In the examination, there will be both an assessor and an interlocutor in the room. The following notes use plural forms where appropriate, although we realise a teacher may often be working alone for practice sessions.

You will need to refer to Paper 5 of Practice Test 4 in the Student's Book and the colour section 'Visual materials for Paper 5' also in the Student's Book.

Phase A   (approximately three minutes)

INTRODUCTIONS

Good morning. My name is ... and this is my colleague ...
And your names are?
First of all we'd like to know a little about you. Do you know each other?

If yes:
In that case, perhaps you (*Candidate A*) would like to tell us a little about (*Candidate B*) – where (s)he's from, what his/her hobbies and interests are, what (s)he does, *etc.*
And (*Candidate B*), would you like to introduce us to (*Candidate A*) now, please?
How long have you known each other?
(*If applicable:*)
What do you know about each other's country?

If no:
Could you please find out about each other? Ask each other where you're from, what you're interested in, how you like to spend your time, why you're learning English, your plans for the future, your families, what you do, *etc.* (*select as applicable*)

GENERAL SOCIAL CONVERSATION

If in UK:
(*Candidate A*), could you tell (*Candidate B*) what it's like to live in ...
(*Candidate B*), do you think you would like to visit ...?
(*Candidate B*), could you now tell (*Candidate A*) about where you live?
How long are you staying here?
Both of you come from places that are rather different from England. What do you think are the biggest differences?
Is there anything in particular that you like or dislike about England? *etc.*

In candidates' country:
Well, you both live here in ... What would you say are the good things about living in ...? Are there any disadvantages?
How do you get to school/work?
What is the best way of travelling round here? *etc.*

Practice Test 4

Phase B (three or four minutes)

1   ROCK BAND (Spot the difference)

In this part of the test I'm going to give you each a picture to look at. Please do not show your pictures to each other.
Indicate rock band picture 4A to Candidate A and rock band picture 4B to Candidate B.
Your pictures are very similar but not the same. I'd like you, (Candidate A), to describe your picture in detail to (Candidate B). Talk about the people and their surroundings. You have about a minute to do this.
I'd like you, (Candidate B), to listen very carefully and then tell us three things which are different in your picture. If you are still uncertain when (Candidate A) has finished, you may ask him/her a few questions to help you.
All right? So, (Candidate A), would you start please?
(Candidate A speaks for approximately one minute.)
Thank you. Now, (Candidate B), can you tell us briefly about the differences you noticed?
(Candidate B speaks for approximately 20 seconds.)
If Candidate B has not identified sufficient differences, ask him/her about some of the similarities.
Thank you very much.
Note: You may wish to allow students to compare their pictures but under examination conditions, candidates would not be invited to compare pictures at the end of this exercise, for security reasons.

2   PICNICS (Describe and relate)

Now I'm going to give each of you a picture to look at. Your pictures are different but they are related in some way. Please do not show your pictures to each other.
Indicate picnic picture 4C to Candidate B and picnic picture 4D to Candidate A.
I'd like you, (Candidate B), to describe your picture to (Candidate A). Describe what's in the picture and say where and when you think it was taken. You have about one minute to do this.
(Candidate A), I'd like you to listen carefully to what (Candidate B) says and afterwards I'd like you to: *(Interlocutor: choose one of the following)*
either spot five things which are the same in both pictures
or spot five things which are different in the two pictures
or say how you think the two pictures are related.
If you are still uncertain when (Candidate B) has finished, you may ask him/her questions to help you. Otherwise I'd like you to say briefly what is the same / what is different / how the pictures are related.
Do you understand? So, would you like to begin please (Candidate B)?
(Candidate B speaks for approximately one minute.)
Thank you. Now, (Candidate A), could you say briefly what is the same / what is different / how the pictures are related?

(*Candidate A speaks for approximately 20 seconds.*)
Thank you very much. Now, would you like to compare your pictures?

Phase C   (three or four minutes)

FUTURE HEADLINES (Discuss)

Indicate the future headlines 4E to the pair of candidates.
I'd like you to look at these headlines and imagine that they might appear in a newspaper in ten years' time. What might be the consequences if any of them were true? Discuss which one would be the most exciting news. You may like to think of others that you would prefer to see.
You have three or four minutes for this.

Phase D   (three or four minutes)

Which headline did you choose as the most exciting? Why?
What do you think might be the consequences if these headlines were true?
Do you think solving one problem might lead to new problems? In what way?
What is the most serious problem facing your part of the world?
Do you have any ideas about how it could be solved?